Shouting Joy to the Storm

Cycle C Sermons for Lent and Easter Based on the Gospel Texts

Schuyler Rhodes

CSS Publishing Company, Inc.
Lima, Ohio

SHOUTING JOY TO THE STORM
CYCLE C SERMONS FOR LENT AND EASTER BASED ON
THE GOSPEL TEXTS

FIRST EDITION
Copyright © 2018
by CSS Publishing Co., Inc.

Library of Congress Cataloging-in-Publication Data

Names: Rhodes, Schuyler, 1953- author.
Title: Shout Joy to the Storm Cycle C sermons for Lent and Easter based on the Gospel texts / Schuyler Rhodes.
Description: First edition. | Lima, Ohio : CSS Publishing Company, Inc., [2018]
Identifiers: LCCN 2018030840 | ISBN 9780788029387 (paperback : alk. paper) | ISBN 078802938X (paperback : alk. paper) | ISBN 9780788029394 (eBook) | ISBN 0788029398 (eBook)
Subjects: LCSH: Lenten sermons. | Easter--Sermons. | Bible. Gospels--Sermons. | Sermons, American--21st century. | Church year sermons. | Common lectionary (1992). Year C. | LCGFT: Sermons.
Classification: LCC BV4277 .R46 2018 | DDC 252/.62--dc23

For more information about CSS Publishing Company resources, visit our website at www.csspub.com, email us at csr@csspub.com, or call (800) 241-4056.

e-book:
ISBN-13: 978-0-7880-2939-4
ISBN-10: 0-7880-2939-8

ISBN-13: 978-0-7880-2938-7
ISBN-10: 0-7880-2938-X   PRINTED IN USA

*This effort is dedicated to the memory of
Daniel Berrigan, SJ, whose love, patience and persistence
taught me how to shout joy to the storm.*

Contents

Introduction

This volume emerges in the midst of vast and seismic change in our world. For good and ill, change is both inevitable and disruptive. Change simply comes. Whether it is in the speed of expanding technology touching daily lives or the instability of politics that seeks division rather than unity — change happens. Change brings delight and it brings pain. What parent does not yearn to hold that infant in his or her arms, forgetting that the baby is now a young adult? Yet, how satisfying it is to build a mature relationship with an adult child? Change. Despite its constant presence, our collective instinct is to do what we can to minimize its pursuant disruption.

This change is so intense that it can feel like we are living in the midst of a violent storm, replete with thunder, lightning, gale force winds and drenching rain. In the midst of this storm there are choices. We can run from it and try to find a dry crevice or cave in which to hide. Or we can stand in the maelstrom and give voice to the joy we have. We can, if we choose, shout joy to the storm.

To rise up in the midst of such force is not an act of futility, as some might suggest. It is, in fact, a step in the direction of salvation. When we stand in the face of the storms of this world, insisting on the powerful joy we have in Christ Jesus, it is both a witness and an act of resistance. Whatever the storm, those around us receive a sense of power from our own testimony to God's power. Whatever the storm, our joy is not diminished. And if the storm is one of injustice, oppression or abuse of power, our voice gives shape to the alternative liberation that comes with God's saving act in Christ Jesus.

So it is that we gather in Christian community to shout like a choir of hope to the storms that buffet us today. To the storm of endless warfare and violence we rise and shout God's word of peace. To the storm of racism and sexism, the tornadoes of division and rancor, we move as community to shout the joyful freedom that comes when we take down the dividing walls between us. And to the storms of our own wounds and pain we lift up the soothing harmonies of hope and new life.

These sermons are not merely the voice of one pastor shouting into the hurricane that howls before us. They are, instead, a piece of the sacred dialogue of Christian community. These words come from the power of planting community gardens at a church in Oakland, California. They come from the rich and wonderful struggles of diverse peoples learning to unwrap the gift of one another's culture. These words dance to the rhythms of faith communities choosing new life rather than stagnation and death. In this brief journey from Lent to Pentecost, it's my profound hope that these pieces of our holy conversation will provide some handle, some hope as each one of us finds ways to shout joy to the storm.

In it all there is no voice that is not significant, no hope that cannot be realized, no vision that God cannot bring to fruition. So take a deep breath as you read, and join the chorus as together we shout God's joy to the storm.

Schuyler Rhodes
Woodland, California

Foreword

Schuyler Rhodes is a writer, a musician, a retreat and workshop leader, a community organizer, a counselor, and a spiritual guide. Through these sermons, the reader will come to appreciate the unique way in which Schuyler brings his multifarious interests, skills, experiences, and talents together to preach the gospel. Schuyler repeatedly tells us in these exhortations that Jesus is what is unique and special about our faith and that his entrance into the world as we know it was the major event in human history. He has been a dynamic and gifted pastor for as long as I have known him — since the early 1980s. He has a big heart, a penetrating gaze, a ready laugh, and deep love for his parishioners and for God. It is with gladness I receive the gift of this collection of his sermons for we live on opposite coasts and I am unable to hear him preach but on the rarest of occasions.

From the beginning of this book, the reader senses that Schuyler Rhodes is an evangelical Christian in the truest sense of the word. He preaches the good news of Jesus Christ. Schuyler loves Jesus and this means he loves justice and peace. They go together and Schuyler has lived out his love for Jesus and justice and peace in a completely authentic manner throughout his distinguished ministry.

Schuyler Rhodes is immensely talented and passionate. Not only is he an acclaimed preacher, he serves as a district superintendent in the United Methodist Church in the California-Nevada Annual Conference and provides leadership for dozens of local congregations and pastors. He works closely with the bishop and other church leaders.

Through these sermons, he reveals his capacity to draw meaning from seemingly mundane activities, from joys and sorrows, from common cares and concerns. These homilies remind us that we truly live out our faith in Christ when we give fully of ourselves, love our neighbors as we love ourselves, offer and seek forgiveness and reconciliation, and truly connect with nature and neighbors.

In a wonderful sense, Schuyler is an 'old-fashioned' preacher in that his sermons include a call to faithfulness, to commitment, to God. Schuyler grew up in the north and has lived in the west, but if he had been a Southern preacher — as my father was — he would have preached at many a revival or camp meeting.

The sermons you will read in this collection deal with real life matters and provide helpful suggestions on how to respond. These sermons emphasize the importance of listening for God's call and how one might respond to it with courage. These sermons are about accountability. They ask people to go deeper, to examine their lives, to live out their commitments to Christ.

These are practical lessons that urge us to wake up and see that the beloved community is here. It is around us and we need to celebrate and participate in it. These are biblically-based sermons that are not afraid of referring to 'politics' and the everyday life taking place around us. They are about fear and security, about temptation and guilt, about choosing a holy way of life and rejecting racism, materialism, and militarism.

Schuyler's sermons are addressed to you and me and to the people who gather in church every Sunday. These are not seminary lectures. Rather, they are based on real life examples, on daily life encounters and interactions. These sermons attempt to answer big questions such as betrayal, authenticity, doubt, cynicism, anger.

Schuyler's not afraid to ask 'Why?' and to wrestle with alternative answers. He doesn't mindlessly parrot traditional explanations and interpretations of scripture. Refreshingly, in these sermons Schuyler takes familiar stories and parables and reimagines them for his listeners. He's not afraid to ask, 'What if?' or to challenge long held assumptions and explanations of biblical passages. He's not shy about sharing his own doubts concerning miracles and doctrines. He doesn't claim to have all the answers and he knows his people have the same questions and doubts.

Schuyler understands that his parishioners need repeated encouragement and support. They need new insights and examples. They need to know the assurance of God's love. They have doubts and questions and they slip and fall. Schuyler has faith in his people. He knows they can do it. They can live faithful lives. He never gives up on them.

But, he continually challenges them. Schuyler is not going to let his people off the hook. Many a sermon has been preached over the centuries that is aimed at affirming the congregation and making them feel good. These are often very popular sermons. It feels great to be told you are a good person and that you have made the right choices and you are leading an honorable life.

It's much harder to have to deal with questions and to have challenges issued, but a faithful Christian pastor cannot avoid doing so. This is courageous. Preachers often cover up their own doubts by proclaiming dogmatic positions in a forthright manner so as to shut off questions and to reinforce doctrinal beliefs or they adopt an omnipotent manner in order to close off debate.

Schuyler is not content with letting his people be content. Life and faith are too important and complicated for that. He knows there is a wide variance between belief and action, between authentic faith and hypocrisy, but he always has hope, hope grounded in Jesus, that we can do better, we can love one another more authentically, we can make it on earth as it is in heaven. These are not grim sermons. Schuyler tells stories, he reminisces, he draws lessons from his life.

Schuyler loves to peel away layers which obscure deeper meanings whether by examining a Hebrew or Greek word and how it has been translated and what it means in the original language or revealing the facile and surface manner in which we live most of our daily lives as opposed to the unvarnished and serious life that Christians are intended to experience.

What Schuyler is continually saying to his congregation is this, "If you're a Christian, live like one." But he's also always reminding his people that Christianity is a communal religion and that we need to be there with and for one another. We must manifest our faith through love in action.

These sermons are not full of platitudes and bromides; rather, although spoken in an encouraging and hopeful manner, they challenge, consistently, the listener. That is preaching as it should be. These sermons call on our better angels. They demand, really, that we abandon cynicism and hypocrisy and small-mindedness, and yet, somehow they also recognize it is in our nature to fall short. We're not perfect, but in a true Wesleyan sense we should seek perfection.

Schuyler's sermons attempt to help people distinguish between wants and needs, love and lust, joy and happiness. They attempt to clarify matters for the reader so that they may better grasp the true meaning of biblical teachings, to put us in touch with signal realities.

These sermons are filled with a sense of wonder. They ask us to look again at familiar teachings and passages with fresh eyes and they ask us to be obedient to the will of God. Many people are dismayed that the community of Christ has failed to be perfect in living out the Gospel and for them this discredits the entire enterprise. Schuyler may feel some exasperation that people don't 'get it', but he doesn't give up on them. He knows we can do better because Christ is in us and with us.

The God Schuyler preaches about is full of understanding, love, and healing, and stands with those who are oppressed and need liberation. Other preachers, many in fact, choose to focus on an angry God who is full of wrath and judgment and doles out punishment. I am grateful Schuyler calls on us to work with God and on behalf of God to bring joy and laughter and justice to the world in which we live.

Because of his own passion for the faith and his love of others, Schuyler continually extends an invitation to his listeners to commit and recommit themselves to God. He continually points people back to the basics of the faith and reminds them it's not about them and their own satisfaction; rather, it's about Jesus and the gift of salvation he offers to us.

— Jim Winkler, President and General Secretary of the National Council of Churches of Christ, USA

Ash Wednesday
Matthew 6:1-6, 16-21

Treasure Hunters

When my children were young, one of the things I loved was preparing treasure hunts for them. I used to spend hours getting ready for these wonderful, rowdy events. Their Mother would take them with her to help with the grocery shopping while I remained home working to lay out a series of elaborate clues. The clues would be written in puzzling rhyme, leading from one place to the next on our five-acre property in the California Sierra Foothills. Clues were hidden in jars buried in the garden, in the neighbors' mailbox, and high up in their favorite climbing tree. They were hidden under the tractor in the shed and tacked to a log in the wood pile. Each clue led them tantalizingly closer to the treasure.

Oh. Right. Treasure.

This is the focus of our scripture this evening, am I right? Well, it's one focus anyway. You know the place, don't you? That place where your heart is located? We'll get there in a moment, but what was the alleged treasure in these elaborate summer games? What could induce kids to spend hours seeking clues and chasing hints? What was the treasure? Well, to be candid, that depended on my mood and sense of humor at the moment. One time the trail of clues led to a tub of hand cranked ice cream in the freezer. On a hot summer day it was received in the same way one would receive gold bullion. Another time the treasure consisted of all the makings for s'mores. For those who may not know, s'mores are a gourmet childhood treat that starts with a roasted marshmallow and a piece of chocolate. These two elements are placed between two pieces of graham cracker to create a sandwich of unparalleled quality. The kids loved them, and still do. There were numerous treasures and I closely followed my own rule that there should no repetition.

Some years later as the children courted young adulthood and had moved beyond such childish pursuits, we were sharing one evening about these treasure hunts. We laughed and reminisced about our beloved house and the time we spent there together. And in the sharing one thing became clear to me. As we shared, I realized that they had no real attachment to, or even a recollection of what the treasures were at the end of these games. No. What was significant for them, what they remembered, was the joy of the chase, the fun of finding the clues and racing on to the next one. It wasn't the prize for them. It was the joy of the moment. It was process, not product.

I remember this with a vivid edge as we dive into this Ash Wednesday text about where exactly our own treasures are located. What, I have to ask, would you name as your treasure? And where would it be found?

When I was a young man my Dad and I built a cabin together on our farm in New York State. It was a family event with uncles and brothers-in-law assisting. I'm pretty sure that it was Dad's way of hoping I'd hang around when down deep he already knew of my wandering spirit. But that cabin we built together was wonderful and over the years it grew. When I met my wife we built an addition and I bought a used piano so she could sit and play her afternoons away. When our kids were born we added a bedroom and bit by bit this project contained and embraced our lives as we escaped the frenzy of urban ministry for some quiet and rest.

The years rolled by with what now feels like a ferocious speed. Then my Dad passed away. It was unexpected and difficult. At about the same time we accepted a posting in California. As these major transitions took hold in our lives, the cabin became a storehouse. It held antiques and family pieces. Crammed into the nooks and crannies were old tables and boxes of trinkets; memorabilia like old post cards and adolescent journals. It even held my great-great grandfather's musket. There were paintings and rugs that went back a hundred years and there were boxes of writings and more.

Then one night some kids broke into the cabin. They got drunk and poured kerosene all over the interior before setting the place on fire, and burning it to the ground. It still tightens my stomach muscles to recall it all. At first I was devastated. This rustic home of dreams, this storehouse of family treasures, had all gone up in smoke. The firemen said it took less than an hour to completely burn. All those years, all those treasures, reduced to cinders in the space of 45 or so minutes? I wafted for some time between anger and sadness — not a great location for one's spirit.

Then it came to me like a holy vision. It was, for me, a God moment. I suddenly realized that, like my children who cherished the search for clues and the treasure hunts, I treasured all the moments I had in that place. No one could burn down the time Dad and I had building that cabin together. No one could strip us of the memories and good times that place held for us. The antiques — even Grandfather's musket — were just things. They were pretty much meaningless things. The treasure was in the love we shared and experienced there, not in heirlooms or property. I had been taught, once again, the lesson of my children and the treasure hunt.

As we step together into this profound time of reflection and self-examination, it might be a good idea for us to think and pray together about where our treasures are to be found. Indeed, what are our treasures? As individuals, what do we value? How do we spend our time? To what, or whom do we give our attention? Where do we spend our resources? The answers to these questions will be informative as we go on this Lenten Journey. This same question comes to us as a faith community. Where is our treasure as church? What is really important to us? And as is the case with us as individual persons, the answer can be found in how we spend our time together. What is it that takes our attention and our focus? Where, precisely, are our hearts as a church? What truly is our treasure?

Are we focused on survival? Are we just a little fearful because attendance is down and the collection is low? Are we waiting for others to come to us and affirm the ways in which we have always been church? Or are we reaching out in love to welcome strangers and share the forgiving grace of the gospel? Is our common heart to be found in the compassion and justice of the living Christ? Or is it mired in the values of our secular culture? I am hoping we will take time in these coming days to ponder and pray about all this.

Friends, not only are we called to engage this as individuals and church, it comes to us to think about our common lives as a nation. In our nation, sisters and brothers, how is it that we spend our time? The average American watches five hours of television a day. Really? Five hours? Apparently this is the case, and some suggest it might be higher than this. These are hours, sisters and brothers, that people used to give to volunteer organizations that focused on improving the wider community. Boy Scouts, Girl Scouts, volunteer fire departments and ambulance services, coaching in community sports programs, Rotary Club, Red Cross; literally hundreds of organizations are starved for volunteer help while the average American watches five hours of television a day. How do we determine our values? Where do we locate our hearts? Where indeed is our treasure?

As we survey the landscape of our lives, this question about treasure becomes a serious one. Where we find our hearts and our treasure has impact far beyond our own individual reality. In a nation that once flourished on volunteerism we struggle with an immature selfishness that borders on narcissism. How can we lead a people to care about others rather than just about themselves? How can we tap into the generous hearts and gracious spirits that are bound up in a world of "fake news" and fear? How can we as a people of faith lead into a tomorrow that is different?

I think the answer to these and many other questions of our day has to do with our ability to live life on purpose. So many of us live our lives as though they will go on forever, allowing noble plans and good intentions to waste away. Our willingness to be intentional about how we live our lives makes a difference. As Christians, do we deliberately schedule time for prayer and bible study? As a people of faith, do we purposefully make time to serve the poor and to give ourselves unstintingly for others? As followers of Jesus, do we pause to see where we might need to offer forgiveness and reconciliation in our own lives and in the life of the wider community?

In the wake of all this I want to call us back to this time of reflection and self-examination, to this Lenten journey we begin this evening. I know that tradition has us giving something up for Lent each year. The symbolism of this is that we surrender something sacrificially to honor and focus upon the sacrifice that will be made for us on the cross on Good Friday. But what if we try something different this year? Instead of giving up coffee or sweets or something like that, what if we commit to a new kind of intentionality in our faith and our lives? Instead of giving something up, let's take on the mutual and powerful commitment of lives lived on purpose in the power and grace of Jesus Christ.

Let us, as we celebrate the Liturgy of the Ashes, take this reminder of mortality as a call to purposeful living. In these coming days let us rise each morning with a plan for faithfulness for the day. Perhaps each day might look something like this as we step out with intention.

1.) We will spend time each day in focused prayer.
2.) We will join or participate in a Bible study here in our church community.
3.) We will commit to giving our time (3 — 10 hours a week) to benefit the wider community.

4.) We will forgive those who have wronged us.

5.) We will seek forgiveness from those whom we have wronged.

These are five things that each of us can do in this season to focus our faith lives and move together to intention and purpose. Perhaps you would want to add something to the list? By all means do so. Yet let us as we prepare to receive the ashes, agree with penitential hearts to commit our Lenten Journey to a more intentional living out of our faith. Let us claim this journey, not for the prize at the end but for its own sake. Let us revel in the gifts we have and claim the love of God in everything we do.

Amen.

Lent 1
Luke 4:1-13

"Until An Opportune Time…"

I need to ask a question this morning. It's a question to which I think I know the answer, but still, I need to ask. Do any of you ever feel tempted? How about a show of hands? Yes, yes, yes. I see that we have a lot of folks being tempted these days. I don't think I will trespass into the question of what exactly tempted you. You can keep that one to yourselves. But truthfully, if we go deeply into this, it's a tough thing to consider, isn't it?

As one who struggles with extra pounds, I am constantly tempted by food that I simply cannot eat. For me, it feels like there is a veritable parade of pastries and pasta, cake and cola, burritos and blintzes, all beckoning me to come and feast. Mmmmm, I love it all, and I simply cannot eat it. Another thing that tempts is procrastination. If I have a project or a thing that needs to get done it's easy for me to delude myself into thinking I can "do it tomorrow." And then suddenly I realize that I will be pulling a couple of all-nighters because I gave into the temptation of something other than what I should have been doing.

And of course, there are more serious temptations. There are temptations that push us on how honest we are; temptations that test us to see how faithful we are to our spouses and partners; temptations that expose our willingness to throw a friend under the bus in order to save our own skin or worse, to make ourselves look good. And of course there are temptations around taxes and tithing, stealing and more. The list is virtually endless, and it is stunning in its variety and complexity.

We live in a torrent of temptation, and our world doesn't help much. How does that advertisement go about Las Vegas? "What happens in Las Vegas stays in Las Vegas?" What does that really mean? It doesn't take a rocket scientist to figure it out, does it? Or consider the car-maker who shall go nameless that trumpets the fact that they "have no boundaries." Oh my. No boundaries? That is dangerous on so many levels. Yet the temptation to push beyond, to transgress boundaries is ever-present, isn't it? Sometimes the boundaries we are tempted to cross are minor, and sometimes they are serious with accompanying consequences. And friends, I don't need to tell you that the world is falling all over its collective commercial impulse to dangle things in front of us; to tempt us into going places we know we shouldn't go. Everyday there are temptations to cheat, to lie, to seek revenge and to manipulate systems in order get what we think we deserve. It is like a vast sea in which we all swim…some better than others.

The world had less technology in Jesus' day but temptation was just as prevalent for him as it is for us today. Think with me about this story. Jesus is tempted by his appetites. The devil says to him, "Go ahead, turn this stone into bread." That's a pretty amazing prospect and one that could even appeal to our fuzzy feel good sense of things. And we know his response, don't we? "One does not live by bread alone." Then of course, comes the lure of power. From the halls of governments to the workings of the Church, power attempts to seduce, and many fall to this temptation. But Jesus resists. "Worship the Lord your God and serve only him..." And lastly Jesus is tempted to test his own divinity by demonstrating immortality in a dramatic leap from the pinnacle of the temple. And still, Jesus resists. "Do not put the Lord your God to the test." And even then, after these extreme enticements, the devil doesn't quit. He merely goes away "until an opportune time."

It seems that the question before us isn't about whether or not we are tempted. The real question has to do with how we respond to temptation. And it is our response to this that creates or destroys us as a people.

It strikes me that there are three basic ways to respond to temptation.

The first is to simply give in to it all in an obfuscating dust-cloud of weak-kneed justification. The language that accompanies this is familiar to us all. "Well, everyone does it...." Or "I'm far from perfect." Or one I heard just the other day, which goes something like this. "Oh, if I don't do it, someone else will step right in and do it themselves. What difference does it make, anyway?" Succumbing to temptation is epidemic in our world. Think for a moment. Do you know someone who surrenders their integrity to temptation and is ready with a carefully constructed defense that articulates why this is reasonable and acceptable? Yes, yes, I think we might indeed know a few folks like that. But before we get too righteous here, let's hold the mirror up for a moment. In what ways have you and I allowed ourselves to float away on the currents of temptation? Where and in what ways do we give ourselves away to lowered expectations and questionable activities? I know. This is difficult. Yet in this season of self-examination such questions are important to pursue.

The second way of responding to temptation is accommodation. Accommodation is the submission to the notion that "it's not really that bad." Even in the moment that this sermon takes shape we can see this in certain peoples' refusal to disavow neo-Nazi and racist rants from hate groups under the guise of something like, "there is hate on all sides." Or worse still is the toleration of genocidal hatred in the name of freedom of speech. This is the attitude that shrugs its shoulders, saying, "If you want to get along you have to go along...." Giving into the temptation to avoid conflict or to wiggle ourselves to a safe distance is wrong. Accommodation as a way of dealing with temptation also allows us to become mired in the swamp of relativity. This is the process of refusing to take a stand and saying that "all points of view are valid."

Friends, let's be clear. If a given point of view leans into murdering whole populations, it isn't a valid perspective to be discussed over tea, it's evil.

The third way of dealing with temptation is the way of Jesus. In the passage before us the devil really puts it to him with some serious moves. This is where we see the mettle of the master as he simply resists. He is offered abundant food when he is famished from fasting. Political power is laid it before him, and the enticing power of his own "equality with God" (Philippians 2:6) is dangled in front of him. Here is our strength and consolation in the struggles we face hourly with temptation. In him there is no surrender or accommodation.

In him the devil is given no quarter. In him there is no interior struggle with the tyranny of his desires (paraphrase from 1 Peter 2:9f). In him is a clear, simple refusal to give in to temptation.

This does not imply that such resistance is easy or even cost free. It takes strength to resist. It takes commitment and clarity to simply say, "No." The good news in this is that Jesus isn't alone in this resistance. Joining him are the likes of St. Francis of Assisi, who surrendered the tempting wealth of family to follow the voice of God; the thousands of Christians, black and white, who participated in the Underground Railroad, resisting the lure of power and the slave economy; Reverend Alex Trocme' of Le Chambon, France, who rather than give in to power and betray his Jewish neighbors to the Nazis, organized his whole parish to assist hundreds of Jews to escape to freedom and new life; Dorothy Day, who founded the Catholic Worker, came to faith later in life and resisted the temptations of hierarchy and power to serve the poor. The list is long and illustrious. It includes the likes of Sojourner Truth, Martin Luther King Jr., Daniel Berrigan, and more. We may tread water in a sea of endless temptations, but we do so in the presence of a mighty cloud of witnesses.

We take heart in the full humanity of Jesus and the many frail, imperfect people who have followed him. We take heart in the support of Christian community who, in prayer, worship and discipline, help us to resist the flood waters of temptation that surround us all. We take heart in the relationships we build together where we support one another in our shared and sacred resistance to the temptations of this world.

Sisters and brothers, in this season let us renew our resistance, to the temptations around us, yes. But let us also renew our commitment to resist evil and oppression wherever we may find it, to regain our stature as ones who will rise up with courage and with the joy we have in our Lord and Savior Christ Jesus.

Amen.

Long View — Long Haul

Have you ever known anyone who has suddenly stopped and changed direction? Maybe it's you. I know that in my life I stopped the pursuit of a career in the theater and finally listened to God's call to me to enter ordained ministry. It wasn't a call, so much, to change direction, as it was a call to authenticity and commitment.

Today, though, I want to tell you about a friend of mine who did this. At the age of fifty, Marcy decided to change everything. She made the momentous decision to leave her job, her home, friends, family and career so she could study medicine so she could go to Central America and work among the poor. Yes, it seemed pretty drastic to us as well.

I mean, this woman was an artist. She was a painter, whose work sold in galleries for tens of thousands of dollars. Her life was established, with great social networks, comfortable routine, reputation and even wealth. She knew who and where she was, and her pervasive air of confidence spoke eloquently to this. This woman had it made.

And yet, out of the blue she called me and asked if we could meet for coffee. I could tell by the tension in her voice that she needed to share something significant. So, a few days later we found ourselves ensconced in a local coffee shop. She put down her coffee cup and looked at me. "I'm going to do it," she said. I blinked in confusion and just a little fearful avoidance. "Do what?" Her gaze was steady and her eyes were dancing. "I am going to go to medical school." You could have knocked me over with a feather.

Understand me now. My friend had even less aptitude for things like chemistry and physics than I have, and that's saying something. She was accustomed to cocktail parties and brunches, staying up late and sleeping late. Nevertheless she had just announced this huge life change. She had actually stopped everything she was doing, and spent some weeks in quiet discernment and listening. In this sacred space she sensed what God wanted for her life, and then, shedding all the fear that most of us wear all the time, she began to take the steps into her new life. She was following a vision. Moreover, she was listening to God.

Our conversation continued for some time as she shared and I asked questions. Then I finally asked, "What was it that caused you to shift like this?" Her reply was…"It's about the long haul."

"The long haul?"

I looked at her with brows furrowed and didn't speak what was on my mind. I kept rolling the phrase over and over in my mind. "The long haul." It presents itself as a quaint phrase, doesn't it? It brings up old wagon trains or overland truck drivers. It conjures up visions of mountain treks and ongoing struggle. When I hear this phrase I imagine black and white images of Humphrey Bogart and Katherine Hepburn going down river in "African Queen."

The long haul.

I wonder what that means for you? What does it mean to consider the long haul in our work or our relationships? In our faith journey? What comes to mind when we think about the big picture in terms of how we live out our lives? Today as we reflect on this gospel passage we see a Jesus who stands his ground in Jerusalem. It doesn't matter if the police are coming to arrest him. He is committed to the work of ministry and neither soldiers nor politicians will stop him. When he is warned of imminent danger, he says, "You go tell that fox that I'll be right here today, tomorrow and the next day." In other words, "You tell that fox that I'm in this for keeps and if he wants to come get me, he knows where I am!" In one sense this is about Jesus throwing down the glove of challenge to his adversary. But in another, deeper sense it is about an abiding commitment.

For Jesus the call to be in Jerusalem was a long haul kind of thing. It's not unlike changing one's life to attend medical school at age fifty. I can hear Marcy now. "You tell all the people who are gossiping about my so called mid-life crisis that I am going to Central America to follow God's call to heal. You tell them that I will be there for the long haul, and they know where to find me."

I don't know about you, but it seems to me that actions like these take courage and clarity. Imagine yourself stopping right now, in this moment, and deciding that you know what God is calling you to do. Imagine knowing God's purpose for your life and no matter what, this is what you're doing to do, and you're going to do it now, not later when it's more convenient. Whether it's staying put in Jerusalem to heal the sick or heading to Managua to work among the poor, you will not be deterred.

What does it take to stand in the shadow of Jesus and dare the authorities to come get you? What does it take to be able to move forward in a specific direction because this is what you are called to do; this is who you are, this the right thing to do and this is the moment to do it. What is it like to stand on the solid ground of commitment? What is it like to have the gift of clarity about God's claim on your life?

It seems to me that such a thing would be both wonderful and terrifying.

How many of us, like my friend who is finishing medical school now, take the time to discern God's call? How many of us simply step out of business as usual to take stock of our lives? How many of us ever journey into the wilderness of our own hearts where we will meet the truth about who we are and who God calls us to become?

I know. I can hear the muted voices in the parking lot now. "I'm not Jesus, you know..." No, none of us are Jesus. But the truth is that we're not called to be Jesus. We are called to be fully ourselves, and it's the discovery of that core reality that I hope will be a piece of our Lenten Journey together. Can we make the commitment to take this precious time to listen for God's yearning for our lives? Jesus stepped away to listen for God's voice. My friend also took a break so she could open her heart to God's claim on her life.

You see, sometimes preparing for the long haul means pacing oneself. Indeed that can be the case. It's important, however, not to confuse a wise and measured stride with a soul killing compromise so we can survive blandly into a future without shape. Gearing up for the long haul doesn't mean melding into a background of meaningless patter. It *does* mean taking the time to be deliberate. It *does* mean taking the care and focus to pay attention. And it does mean lasting, persistent, even stubborn commitment.

In this time of winter blahs and burn-out; in these days of frenzy and over-work; in this season of broken promises and unmet commitments, each one of us is beckoned — called — begged by the Holy Spirit to slow down and stop. And having ceased our perpetual motion, we are urged to put our hands together and listen in prayerful silence for the wonder of God's claim upon our lives.

We are literally touched by God's desire in this moment; by God's deep love and longing for each person, for each relationship, for each community. It is all here — now.

And in grace and hope, in understanding and compassion, in authenticity and power, this Lenten moment touches us. As we prepare for God's sacrifice, let us shed the swarming intensity of life's manifold distractions and listen. Listen. Listen for the voice of the Holy — the gentle, challenging, comforting call for the long haul.

Amen.

One More Year

Have you ever been judged and found wanting? No? Well, I have. I remember about a thousand years ago when I first went off to college. It was a heady time. I had grown up in a fairly controlled environment and the sudden surge of freedom caused me to, well, go a little crazy. I will be honest with you. I did more partying than I did studying. The result of this was that I was soon on academic probation. Moreover, I got called into the academic dean's office for what was called a "conversation." I showed up at the appointed hour and was made to wait for another forty minutes just to be certain we knew who was in charge here. Then I was ushered into the dean's office. She was busy reading my file with a terse look on her face that was perfectly accented by reading glasses that sat just a little too far down on her nose. She arched her eyebrows and looked up at me. "Well, we have been enjoying our first semester at school, haven't we?" The use of the word "we" was confusing. I had not seen her at any of the parties I had attended unless she was carefully disguised. I stuffed my resentment down and mumbled, "Yes Ma'am."

I don't think she liked being called "Ma'am. She did her own stuffing down of resentment and continued. "You know this cannot continue, don't you Mr.

Rhodes?" Yes, that had occurred to me. "You are occupying a space in this institution, which means someone else did not get accepted. Why should we allow you to take up space without you performing in ways that we know you can?" I said nothing, but my flushed, embarrassed face spoke volumes. She sighed and said, "Well, it took you some weeks to get into this spot. I suppose we can give you the same amount of time to get out of it. But understand this. You could find yourself expelled if you do not improve."

I think you could say that she lit a fire under me. I did not wish to be expelled for a host of reasons, not the least of which would be explaining this to my mother and father. So, I did a lot less partying and a lot more studying, and by the end of the semester I had pulled my grades up to a respectable level. I went on to graduate with a passable "B" average.

This parable we just heard has a measured kind of rhythm to it. It is not unlike the academic dean at my school. She had the capacity to mix grace with accountability. The man had been waiting three years to get some fruit from his fig tree and was understandably a bit frustrated. He instructed that gardener to cut it down because it was wasting soil. The gardener, though, called for grace, asking for one more year and a bit of fertilizer. Like most parables, there are few if any answers given. We don't know, for example, if the land owner allowed for another year. And if he did allow for it, we don't know if the tree produced any fruit. What is presented here is not a story with solutions but a tale with possibilities.

Are there places in your life where you, like the fig tree, are not producing fruit? My guess is that most of us could answer this in the affirmative. In the landscape of our lives there are many places where it's important to be fruitful. From parenting to work to school and back again, we are called to be fruitful. And if we are continuously unable to produce fruit, there are often consequences, aren't there? In my case, I could have easily found myself on the bus back home. In the case of the fig tree the consequences could range from being immediately cut down to having a year to get it together. I think of all the areas of our lives where fruitfulness is important. You can think of these things as well, I know. But for now, let's focus on what this means for our faith community.

What does it mean for a faith community to bear fruit? And then, sisters and brothers, what does it mean for us if we are not bearing fruit?

Let's take the first question first. One obvious answer to that is that we should be growing. We should not be growing, sisters and brothers, just so we can increase numbers and revenue. No. We should be growing because the kind of community we offer here is not offered elsewhere. If we are fruitful, our Christian community is loving, gracious, affirming, and transformative. If we are fruitful, we are the kind of community that offers God's incredible love and grace to everyone. We should be adding souls to the life of the community because people out there truly need the healing love of Christ. On top of that, friends, the world needs you. It's true. And we cannot dodge the fact that a significant part of our work as a Christian community is to invite and welcome people into discipleship and relationship, both with God and all of us! So let me ask the question. How are we doing on that score? Do we need to dig around the roots a bit? Add some fertilizer? I love the possibility and the potential that can come when we blend accountability with grace.

Another key factor of Christian community is the quality of our relationships with one another. Our call is to be loving and forgiving, to be mutually supportive and to create safe space for everyone. In this "sanctuary" people should be safe in their spirit so that they can explore their faith in God. They should also feel safe in their hearts. That is, free from gossip and negative talk. In Christian community if we talk about someone else, it is only to lift that person up to God's glory. No one should ever feel the sting of parking lot gossip or innuendo. And finally, people should be physically and emotionally safe. That means our facilities should be in good condition, and it means that we should have good, healthy boundaries around sexual and other concerns. The same question arises. How are we doing on that score?

Sisters and brothers, another unavoidable piece of being fruitful in Christ is our willingness to stand with the poor and the oppressed, and to work for peace in our world. I know. Some of you are sitting there thinking that the pastor is getting all political again. Friends, let us make a clear distinction between the gospel call to serve the poor and to be peacemakers, and partisan political positions. Living out the gospel will always have political implications, it's true. But that is a substantially different thing than staking out an ideological position in church. Remember this. In this church community there is no right wing or left wings, the only sound you will hear in this congregation is the sound of angel's wings. We do our level best in this church to follow the way of Jesus. I think not of political sides but of the voice of scripture saying, "if you did not do it to the least of these, you did not do it to me." (Matthew 25:45-46) So, with that said, the same question comes. How are we doing on this one?

We've taken a moment to think about what fruitfulness looks like. Now we should think together about what happens if we fail to be fruitful? What if the gardener talked the landowner into giving him a year to work with the fig tree and we simply don't bear fruit? What happens if we do not bear the fruit of discipleship and the building up of community? What happens if we are mean and spiteful to one another and to others who come to us? And what happens if we do not feed the hungry, heal the sick, and follow the way of Jesus? What are the consequences of not bearing fruit?

John Wesley, who founded the movement that became the Methodist Church, said that he wasn't so much afraid of the people called Methodist ceasing to exist. His real fear was that they would become a hollow shell bearing the form but none of the substance of Christian community. His real fear was that they would become dead in the faith. This could be one consequence of not bearing fruit.

Another consequence comes from the fact that people watch us. They know who we are and what we say we believe. And if our words and our lives do not cohere, then the world out there ceases to take us seriously and we become a kind of joke that is too stale to even tell anymore. If we are not fruitful, we become irrelevant.

The good news, though, is that we are called to live into the tension between accountability and grace. We are called to honesty and truthfulness about where we are doing well and where we could use improvement.

And friends, we are called above all else to be faithful in following the path of Jesus.

I believe that we should add these questions to our ongoing Lenten reflection and self-examination. Are we bearing fruit as Christian community? Are we creating disciples of Jesus? Are we students of the master? Are we creating a community that is a safe space for all people? Are we living out the teachings of the master? Are we serving the poor? Are we being witnesses for peace? What do you think? In some areas, we're doing well. In others we could use a little help.

As we pray and consider all this, I am wondering what it looks like for us to dig around the roots a little? How can we freshen and fertilize the soil of this Christian community so that we might better bear fruit? How is it that we can find this balance of accountability and grace within our community and with one another?

My earnest hope and my personal commitment is that we will partner together as we work to bear the fruit of faithfulness. My ongoing prayer and deepest desire is that we will give ourselves the Lenten gift of accountability and grace as we speak truth and create space for growth and change.

Amen.

They Should Have Fired
That Shepherd

Not too long ago I had the privilege of being invited to preach at a conference in a different part of the country. I had a great conversation with the organizer of the conference, bought my plane ticket, and headed to my destination. After landing safely, I retrieved my luggage and went to meet my host. I had seen her photo before, and she gave me a description of her and what she would be wearing. No sweat, right? Then, after a few minutes I saw her. I stuck up my arm and waved, calling her name. Her face brightened up and she waved back, heading in my direction. "This is good," I thought, "right on schedule!"

My host came across the large room and as she got closer I stuck out my hand and said, "It's so great to meet you!" But she walked right past me and hugged a guy behind me, gushing, "I missed you so much! I'm so glad you're home!"

Boy was I embarrassed! Of course, she didn't even notice me! She didn't know me! I had thought all the time that she was waving to me, coming over to greet me, but nope. She zoomed past me like I didn't even exist. I know. It's my problem, not hers. And besides, it's not that big a deal, right? Still, that experience has stayed with me, not so much because I was embarrassed, though that was certainly the case. No, I think it has stayed with me because it hit me that what I perceived to be real, wasn't necessarily real. I was sure this woman was my host. But no, not even close. Reality isn't just my point of view or my experience, is it?

Has anything like this ever happened to you? You are quite sure that you have a handle on what's taking place. You know what's going on, and you understand everything, until of course, you don't.

It's like the time I was trying to help this guy park his car. I was coming out of the store and I saw him there jockeying back and forth without having any luck getting his car into that tight parking spot. So I walked right on over and waved as I started directing him into the spot. "Just a little to the left! That's right. Now straighten your wheels. You got it!" And just like that, he was in his parking spot. He leaned out the window of his car and I went over to say, 'Hello'." He was grinning a little sheepishly as he shook my hand. He said, "Thanks for the help. I really appreciate it. But I was trying to get *out* of that parking spot, not into it."

I think that all too often we fall into the glue of our own perceptions and we get stuck there, unable to hear a fresh point of view. It's for moments like this that Jesus offers his parables.

Jesus comes to us today with stories that, by anyone's accounting, are simply strange. Many of us are used to hearing these stories and we seldom stop to really examine them. So let's review them for a moment. We have three parables today. The Parable of the Lost Sheep, the Lost Coin, and the Prodigal Son.

The parable of the lost sheep has a shepherd losing one lamb out of a whole flock of sheep. This shepherd then left that entire flock unguarded, uncared for, and unattended while he wandered off in search of the lost one. It's important to realize that shepherding in first-century Palestine was a tough job. There were poachers as well as natural predators. You have to add to this the fact that sheep just aren't too bright. Being a shepherd is not an easy job, and one of the key expectations is that you are to return the flock for shearing and butchering with as many as you took out to pasture.

So when one lamb goes missing, does it make sense to risk the whole flock to find that one? No. It's a regrettable loss but that's how it goes. Right? You stick around and give your attention to the whole flock, not just one lamb with a bad sense of direction. Think about it. If this story took place in what we like to call the "real world," that shepherd would have been fired instantly. Even if he didn't lose any of the herd while he was off trying to find the one who wandered off, his irresponsibility in leaving the majority unattended would have been enough to terminate him because he just might do it again.

If it was my flock, I'd fire him.

Then we get to this ridiculous woman and her lost coin. Let's look at this carefully. This woman lost a coin. She spent a whole day looking for it and eventually found the coin. No big deal so far. Then, however, she called everyone over to have a party to celebrate finding the coin! My guess is she spent much more than the coin was worth on the wine and food for the celebration! I do not understand this! Why not just get a piggy bank, put the coin in there and leave it there. Losing a coin and then after finding it, spending it to have a party to celebrate the finding makes me shake my head in confusion.

And finally we get to the parable of the Prodigal Son. In this story we have a wealthy man and two sons. One of the sons asked for, and received his inheritance early. He left town and headed to the big city where he led a dissipated life and blew the whole amount. In fact, he sank so low that he was eating out of dumpsters in back of McDonald's and sleeping on a park bench. As his quality of life continued to decline it dawned on him that even his father's hired hands had a place to sleep and enough to eat. He decided to go home and throw himself on his father's mercy, asking him to be treated like a hired hand. At least then he wouldn't starve.

Well, Dad saw him coming way off in the distance. Instead of being upset, he was overjoyed. He killed the fatted calf and put on a party to welcome the wayward son home. Meanwhile, the good son, the dutiful son, the one who stayed home, and didn't ask for his inheritance, was watching all this take place. As you may imagine he was not too happy. He was the loyal, hard-working one. He stayed home to help and do what was expected of him. Then this ne'er do well came home after blowing his whole inheritance and was welcomed like royalty. Really? No one threw a big party for the loyal one who stayed home.

Most of us have at least a passing acquaintance with these stories. Perhaps we know them well enough that we have come to a point where we let them flow over us like a tepid stream of air that we barely notice. But the truth is that these are the stories of lunatics. Jesus tells us these stories and dangles bizarre situations and untenable story lines in front of us and they simply make no sense in the world in which we live.

What, I wonder, as we travel this Lenten road together, do these stories call us to consider? Are we to abandon our responsibilities and wander off in search of the lost? Are we to go out and spend fifty dollars on a party to celebrate the fact that we found a quarter? Do we ignore the good and faithful people in our lives when someone who has cheated, stolen from us, and hurt us returns to ask for more?

Yes.

Yes, and yes. You see, these stories come to meet us like that woman at the conference who didn't quite come for me. Like the guy that was trying to get out of the parking spot, these stories conspire to invade our sense of the way things are, challenging us to open our imaginations to the way things might be in the kingdom of God. It is in the parables of Jesus that we discover the almost unfathomable notion that in the love of God in Jesus Christ, all bets are off.

As I consider the parables of Jesus I find myself drawn to the old hymn by Isaac Watts titled "When I Survey the Wondrous Cross."

When I survey the wondrous cross
On which the Prince of Glory died;
My richest gain I count as loss,
And pour contempt on all my pride.

I love that hymn, but then I meditate on the words and I can't help myself. The wondrous cross? It is a notion similar to what we see in the parables. The cross isn't wondrous. It's an instrument of state execution on which the Savior of the world was horribly murdered. We are once again called upon to let go of our preconceived notions. We are called to abandon that which we think is real and open our hearts and our minds to God's kingdom, where everything is turned upside down.

The prevailing wisdom that says we can sacrifice one or a thousand for the alleged good of the many is to be called into question and challenged. Jesus, in this parable about a lost lamb, calls us to the particularity of sacred love. Each one matters, which means that you matter. The ridiculous notion that the ends justifies the means runs smack into the heart of a mighty Savior who tell us that in him, the means are the ends. The means are the ends.

In the Parable of the Lost Coin we discover that in Christ, the joy of being together in love and celebration is more important than the resources it takes to be there. Community is what matters. You, the Body of Christ, in this time and place are not only what matters, you are the hope of the church. So we celebrate the love and the hope, the trust and the integrity we find in ministry. In this ministry, sisters and brothers, we will spend more than we have. We will dare to spend ourselves and take great risks to open the gates of love, the doors of wonder, the windows of light, and new life in Christ.

Together, we will also make ourselves ready to greet the prodigal son, in whatever shape he or she arrives as we say "yes" to God's forgiveness and grace.

Each of these stories reaches out to us and challenges our understanding of what is real. Each of these parables turns our world inside-out and bids us take another look at life. Indeed, the call of these stories and the call of Jesus is to collaborate with him in the building of a new reality; a place where abundant generosity and hope are the norm, a place we know as the kingdom of God.

Amen.

You Will Always Have
The Poor With You...

Have you ever been in a situation where you have said something that got totally misunderstood? I remember once some years ago there was a horrible fire in a church in the community where I was serving. This fire burned the centuries old church to the ground. It was a beautiful example of older architecture and the people of the congregation loved the place. The truth, though, was that the congregation was in decline and it seemed like closure of the church was imminent. However, the fire did something. Suddenly, people emerged from everywhere, as the worship services moved across town to the high school gym. The choir grew, attendance surged and this church suddenly, inexplicably, took on a fresh spirit and new life.

One day a year or so after the fire, the chair of the church council was heard to say that maybe the fire was a good thing. Well, the rumor mill took about three hours to spread the story that the church council chairperson was glad that there was a fire. There was high drama all around and it took the pastor months to calm the situation created by a completely misunderstood comment.

Of course, we should all take care in what we say and how we say it, but the truth is that people will always have their interpretations. The same is certainly true with holy scripture. Let's look at two places in the Bible where popular interpretations get spun out of Jesus' teachings with the resultant understandings landing far from the core of the gospel. One of these is in Mark 12:13-17 when the Pharisees try to trap Jesus, asking him if it's lawful to pay taxes. Jesus' famous response is: "Give to the emperor the things that are the emperor's and to God the things that are God's." For many, the popular interpretation of this passage is that it's proof positive that good Christians should pay their taxes. How many of you have heard this? However, if you take a closer look at the context of the passage, we discover that Jesus is not saying that at all. Any good Jew of Jesus' day knew that everything belongs to God — everything. "The earth is the Lord's and everything in it..."(Psalm 24:1). So Jesus, rather than approving the payment of taxes was making a very shrewd response with which the Pharisee's could not argue. From Jesus' point of view, nothing belongs to the emperor. It all belongs to God. This is why scripture says that the people were "utterly amazed" (Mark 12:17b).

We find a similar kind spin on our passage for today. Jesus is at a dinner party at the home of Lazarus, "whom he raised from the dead." (John 12:1b) Consider this setting! Everyone there knew the power of the master. He had raised Lazarus, after all! And now they are together at the table, knowing full well the power of the one who is sitting with them. It must have been an incredible moment. So Mary takes the expensive perfume and anoints Jesus' feet. The exchange is familiar to us. Judas challenges this, claiming that the money could have been given to the poor. Jesus responds.

"Leave her alone. She bought it that she might have it for the day of my burial. You always have the poor with you, but you do not always have me."

A common and oft heard interpretation of this passage is that Jesus said there would always be poor among us, so why should we waste our time on a problem that will always be with us? After all, Jesus said so. Friends, rest assured that Jesus was not justifying poverty or relieving us of our responsibility for ending it. The passage draws attention to Jesus' impending death and the perfume is a symbolic enactment of a funeral ritual. In this passage, the call comes in love and abundant compassion to receive the giver of life and to embrace the gift of the resurrection, even as Lazarus himself is embraced in table fellowship. To put it more simply, our call is not to take our eyes off the ball. In this case, the ball is Jesus, whose teaching, life, death, and rising call us to lives of holiness and hope. So if we are trying to focus on Jesus and the cynical distractions of Judas come at us, hear the words of the master. "Leave her alone."

The question of focus and clarity arises in all this. Let us ask ourselves. Do we have our eyes on the ball? Are we truly focused on living out the gospel of Jesus? Or are we distracted by culturally moderated interpretations of scripture designed to support secular culture rather than lead us to faithful living? Let us think together about our lives as Christian community. Are we focused on ministry? Or do we use our faith to support our particular ideology or world-view?

In many places, our churches are fighting the so-called culture wars between liberals and conservatives. I know this because I have witnessed it across our nation. Yet think a moment. When we allow ourselves to be divided by such categories are we keeping our eye on the ball? When scriptures tell us we are "one in Christ" (Romans 12:5, Galatians 3:28), yet we separate ourselves along the lines of our allegedly important issues, are we not being distracted? No one ever said that we would or should be in agreement on everything. But scripture is clear that we are to be one body in Christ. Our unity, sisters and brothers, does not emerge from things upon which we find agreement, but upon our common membership in Christ's body.

Fully aware of this, the powers of this world attempt to divide us into camps (Ephesians 6:12f). Everyone who agrees with this goes on one side. Everyone who disagrees with it goes on the other. The truth is life isn't that simple. My wife always tells me that I was a great liberal until our daughter was born. Then things changed a bit. We are all complex and wonderfully made beings and to split us into narrowly defined adversarial groups who bicker and whine at one another does not advance the gospel of love...does it?

We are taught to conduct our lives by connecting only with those things and people who agree with us, and this toxic rending of community hurts not only us, but everyone on every side of our self-important concerns. I remember selecting a particular book for a church book study I was leading. The author of this book had a wide reputation as a conservative. At the first meeting a number of people in the group objected loudly saying, "We can't read this book!" I assembled a strategically puzzled look on my face and said, "Why?" The somewhat aggressive, angry leader of this group looked sternly at me and said, "We don't agree with it." My puzzled look deepened. "Then you have read this?" The response was quick. "No! He is a conservative! We don't agree with him so we won't read this book!"

Friends, we must learn to experience points of view beyond our own if we are to keep our eye upon the Christ who calls us, not to division, but into relationship with one another. The temptation to sequester ourselves in the cloistered room of our own opinions turns us into that Judas who jumped on Mary with a quick accusation. "That money could have been given to the poor!" And one must admit that there is some credence to this, until we look deeper into the story and reality of the resurrection live. Jesus says, "Leave her alone. You always have the poor among you, but you do not have me." He rebuts Judas, trying to get him to keep his eyes on the ball.

As we move toward Jerusalem and Palm Sunday, it's important that we come together as a people of Christ to build a community that can maintain its focus on love, compassion, and hope. It's important that we keep our eyes on the ball. And as we keep our eyes on the prize, let us remember our call is not to agreement on issues, but to unity in Christ. Let us remember to rise above the forces that would divide us. Let us take a seat at the table with Lazarus who has been raised from the dead and with Jesus as Mary prepares him for what must come. Let us clasp hands and hearts as we rise above cynicism and walk toward Jerusalem together.

Amen.

Liturgy of the Palms
Luke 19:28-40

I Love A Parade!

I wonder how many of you love parades? I think most of us get excited about a parade with all the people marching down the streets with the bands and the floats and different community groups marching. It's a time of big celebration. When I used to serve a church in New York City it seemed like there were always these huge parades. There was the Macy's Thanksgiving Parade and the Halloween Parade down Sixth Avenue in Lower Manhattan. There were parades for Cinco de Mayo, Saint Patrick's Day, Gay Pride, for all the national holidays, and more. There were also some highly charged religious and political parades. When you gather six million people in one place there's generally no shortage of reasons to start marching down the street.

Each parade had its own special character. Of course, the Macy's Parade was the kick off to the holiday shopping season. We used to love to watch the giant inflated floats as they went by in a halting kind of glory. I think my favorite was the giant Snoopy from the "Peanuts" comic strip and cartoon. The parade was truly amazing because high school marching bands and honor guards from around the country would participate. There were even floats with the casts from Broadway musicals singing their way down the street.

It was, and remains a true spectacle as the city and the nation stepped into the "Christmas Season."

The Saint Patrick's parade was a little different, of course. This celebration of all things Irish had bagpipes and kilts and the firm commitment that for one day, everyone was a little Irish. The Gay Pride parade was always loud and flamboyant as a people too long oppressed geared up for an out loud march with outlandish costumes, music, and dancing. And then, of course, if the Mets or the Yankees won the World Series there was a big parade then as well.

Of course, some of the more jaded New Yorkers didn't like all the parades. Their claim was that these events interrupted routine, caused traffic jams, and brought all those people in from out of town. They pointed out, too, that often the parades were an excuse for public drunkenness and bad behavior. You can bet that folks from the neighborhood were not wild about that. Indeed, this was a favorite rant among some of the members of my parish in Lower Manhattan.

There was one parade, though, that rose above all the others. There was one time when an entire city banded together and celebrated with pure abandonment and joy. This was the day that New York welcomed Nelson Mandela after his release from prison where he was held for twenty-seven years because he was guilty of working to liberate his people. After only four months of freedom, Mandela was greeted by more than a million people in the streets of New York City. On June 21, 1990, this man who gave his life for his nation was given a hero's welcome in our country. I will never forget the roaring cheers that echoed across New York City. I was standing wedged in between countless strangers cherishing this glimpse of greatness as it passed. My heart was filled. I found myself covered in ticker-tape and sobbing on the curb after the parade had moved on uptown. I was not sad or upset. These were tears of joy. My tears came because it was clear that there is true goodness in this world. The tears running down my face came because with Mandela's sacrifice we learned that great things are still possible.

Friends, I confess that I often think of President Mandela on Palm Sunday. Somehow I cannot help imagining a similar kind of energy in Jerusalem that day. In my heart I sense that the intensity and roar of the crowd I experienced in 1990 had the same quality as when Jesus passed by riding a donkey with people shouting "Hosanna!" and paving the street with their clothes. Unlike the numerous other parades I've experienced, these were not giant, rowdy parties rolling down the street, though they surely were loud. These were not events anchored around politics or national pride, though political implications were abundant. No, Palm Sunday in Jerusalem two millennia ago and June 21, 1990, in New York shared from a deeper well than the Macy's or St. Patrick's Day Parades.

There are those among us who lead, not merely with words, but with their lives. This was true of Mandela, and it was certainly true of our Lord and Savior. In Jerusalem on that day the joy and the power of Jesus' ministry was so palpable, so inspiring that he could not bid them be quiet because if they were, "even the stones would cry out..."

The truth for us, though, is that we know how these two stories go, don't we? Nelson Mandela has passed away and his beloved South Africa struggles still to attain justice, equity and freedom for all. And we know all too well what follows the Palm Sunday parade in Jerusalem. Indeed, I wonder if we indeed know too well what is to follow. Even though an empty tomb awaits us, I wonder if we are so used to this story that it's hard for us to seize any one moment and simply savor it.

It strikes me that our full embrace of the Palm Sunday experience is always tempered by what happens in the garden as Jesus is betrayed and hauled off to be tortured and finally executed. It's like the person who is always convinced that something bad is coming down the road. Maybe you know someone like this? People like this are so focused on the bad thing that may be coming that they rob themselves of the beauty of the moment in which they currently exist. Sure, we know the story. Let us remember, though, that all those people waving palm branches and shouting praise did not know. They were there, in power, for the moment, for the reality of the coming Messiah.

So what about us? What about now? Right now? Right this minute let us give ourselves to the enthusiasm of the parade. Let us revel in joy as our master arrives with power and we feel lifted by angels wings as we join the chorus singing, "Hosanna, hosanna! Blessed is the one who comes in the name of the Lord!"

This is our challenge, not only today, but in the whole of our lives.

How often is it that we rob ourselves of the joy of the present moment because we are anxious about the future? How many times do we keep ourselves from stepping into something new because we are afraid we might fail? And how often, sisters and brothers, do we not even get up to go to the parade because we are weary or cynical, or convinced that nothing good can emerge in the midst of our present crises?

My friends, I am not in the habit of giving advice. It usually is either the subject of humor, or it is ignored. So in trepidation I offer this. Don't stay home from this parade. This parade is one you won't regret attending. For this parade you need to lean into enthusiasm and optimism. In order to go to this parade you need to check your bag of cynicism at the door. In order to stand and cheer in this crowd it's necessary to reach beyond oneself. On this Palm Sunday let us go to the parade and stand with the throng. Let us throw our coats in the roadway and wave the palms shouting "Hosanna! Hosanna! Blessed is the one who comes in the name of the Lord!"

Amen.

Dirty Feet

When I was a kid, we spent our summers on the family farm in upstate New York. We would leave as soon as school was out at the end of June and remain there in a state of liberated bliss right through the Labor Day weekend. We were liberated in lots of ways. The family farm had over a hundred acres over which we could freely roam. We built forts and went swimming in the creek that ran through the property every day. We picked wild berries and even grudgingly submitted to weeding my Dad's beloved vegetable garden. If the truth were told, though, the weeding seemed less onerous when we were gnawing on a butter drenched ear of fresh corn.

But of all the bits and pieces of summer freedom there was one that stood head and shoulders above the rest. This was better than campfires and roasted marshmallows. It was light years ahead of climbing trees, and it was by far the most coveted piece of summer. This piece of summer glory was the simple fact that for nearly two months we did not have to wear shoes. From the time we arrived at the farm, with brief interludes for church and such, until we headed home at the end of August, we were outrageously and unashamedly barefoot.

There was real joy in being barefoot. We squished through the mud of July rainstorms and scuffed in the dust of high noon heat. Our feet got scuffed and scraped, cut and bruised, and still we would not surrender to the oppression of socks and sneakers. It is a memory that I cherish and share with my siblings when we gather.

The one thing about going barefoot that must be confessed, however, is that feet get dirty — really dirty. Feet get so dirty that it is possible to wonder whose feet those are under the layers of dried mud and grime. The only way the feet get cleaned is by going swimming of course — or better yet having your Mom wash your feet with a cloth and the garden hose. When this happens you squirm and pretend displeasure but no one is fooled. It's an amazing thing to see the rivers of dirt flow from the feet as water is poured over them. It feels good to have the wash cloth chase the dirt away in sheets of cascading water. And when it's your mother tending to the task, it takes a deeper and tenderer tone. It is an act of selflessness, a labor of love.

But let's jump back a couple of millennia. Let's try to inhabit the story we see unfolding here in the gospel of John. Unlike my halcyon days of summer, Jesus and his pals didn't have the luxury of choosing to go barefoot. Footwear for these guys was sandals, and sandals only. Indeed, sandals implied an economic location in themselves. Many people did not even have sandals. Dirty feet at the end of a long journey bore no resemblance whatsoever to the thrill of adolescent rebellious joy of gooey mud between the toes. In fact, the task of cleaning travel weary feet did not fall to the loving attention of someone's mother. It fell to a servant, one of lower station and social consideration. The people who washed your feet were not worthy of conversation. They were merely objects trained to meet the needs of their superiors. Often, in these times of Roman occupation, those who washed your feet were not just servants. They were slaves.

Thus, when Jesus prepared to wash his disciples' feet it was not merely shocking, it was unimaginable. Violating convention, culture and practice, all which were very deeply rooted in the collective consciousness, Jesus embodied the words that Paul wrote later in his letter to the church in Philippi:

> *Let this same mind be in you that was in Christ Jesus, who though he was in the form of God did not count equality with God as something to be exploited, but emptied himself, taking the form of a slave.* (Philippians 2:5-7)

Of course, Peter reacts. Peter was, I think it's safe to say, a reactive personality. Peter says, "Are *you* going to wash *my* feet (emphasis mine)?" We can only mine the genuine shock and surprise from the context. Jesus, teacher, master, Messiah, is about to debase himself by performing the task of a slave. It is more than Peter can absorb. Even after the ever patient Jesus basically says, "Don't worry, you may not get this now but you will understand it later," Peter launches with the emotional outburst, "You shall never wash my feet!"

Emerging from a culture of hierarchy and rigid social categories, Peter has understandably placed Jesus pretty high up on the ladder. It is beyond his grasp that Jesus should even consider something so beneath him, and it isn't until Jesus gets clear that Peter begins to comprehend what is happening. Jesus says, "Unless I wash you, you have no share in me." Wow. It could not be much more clear. Unless we accept the ministry of Jesus as a servant ministry we have no real part in it.

Unless we ourselves become servants, debasing ourselves in service of others, we really do not participate in the ministry of Jesus. Unless we pour ourselves out for others as Jesus did for us, we are missing the mark.

How difficult that must have been for Peter to fathom. How difficult, one is led to ask, it is for us? Do we, like Peter, place Jesus on a pedestal high above us and worship some idolatrous image that is nothing like him? I don't know about you, but I heard throughout my young life that "Jesus was perfect," and I could never hope to emulate him. Really? Perfect? Such a notion is not only wrong, it is beside the point. Jesus came among us to show us a way of compassion love and servanthood; a way of life that is rooted in giving oneself for others. This is why it is so significant that on this night Jesus takes off his robe and grabs a towel and begins to wash the feet of his disciples.

Tonight, as we engage in this ancient ritual of foot washing, let us remember several things. As we come, let us remember dirty feet. Not the soiled toes of childhood romps in the woods but the filthy feet of weary travelers. Let us conjure up feet that are stained and filthy from miles on dusty roads. Let us imagine tired feet, weary feet. And sisters and brothers, let us remember that what we undertake this night is the work of servants and slaves; the ministry of caring for and serving one another.

In this powerful moment let each one of us claim anew our call to servant ministry and to self-giving love. Let us go where Peter finally went, saying "not my feet only but my hands and head."

Amen.

What Is Truth?

Tonight we gather in darkness to hear a tale of darkness. It is, for many of us, a familiar story. This is the story of the arrest, torture, and execution of Jesus. It is a difficult and bloody narrative that concludes this night with his being laid in the tomb and with each one of us praying and processing what all this means in this time and this place. I know. For some, the mention of the word, "politics" from the pulpit is troublesome. But friends, let us be clear and unambiguous. This was a political execution. Jesus was set up as a would-be "King of the Jews" and neither Jews nor Romans were eager for competition in the power game. So Jesus got eliminated.

In order for such a process to proceed, however, it was important that a narrative be constructed that met the needs of the "principalities and the powers (Ephesians 6:10f)," who cared less about truth than they did about domination and power. So it was that the famous conversation between Jesus and Pilate took place with words that could be issuing forth from the tweets of certain leaders even today.

Jesus was being abused and shuffled between the religious authorities and the state authorities and found himself finally in Pilate's presence. The conversation didn't go well. It began with Pilate asking Jesus if he's "King of the Jews." Jesus, with what could be discerned as sarcasm says, "Do you ask this on your own, or did others tell you about me?" Pilate retorts, and I paraphrase, saying that he's not a Jew and points out that it's his own people who want him eliminated. And Pilate pushes Jesus with the question, "What have you done?"

It's the usual question spat out by those who assume that if you get arrested and find yourself in front of the interrogator that you must be guilty of something. From the Gestapo to our own immigration police, to local police rounding up African American young men, the presumption of guilt accompanies all who are seized. Jesus, nonetheless persisted, pointing out that his alleged kingdom was not a kingdom like Rome or even the temple authorities. But Pilate pressed him saying, "So, you *are* a king?" Jesus proceeded to point out that it was Pilate who was calling him a king, it was not a title Jesus sought or used. Jesus summed up his defense saying he was born to testify to the truth. Then Pilate in words that were both ancient and achingly contemporary said, "What is truth?"

I hear these words, and I cannot unhear all the cries swirling in our current malaise about "fake news" and "alternative facts." The parallelisms here are stunning. It is a trick as old as time. Confuse, malign, and obfuscate by pretending that truth doesn't actually exist. Dismantle the carefully woven constructs of consensus and covenant and pit the people against one another so that they will not notice what authority is doing.

Pilate aimed the question like a weapon. "What is truth?" It was asked as though every simpleton knew that there was no real discernible answer. It was asked with the bullying swagger of the authoritarian whose cynicism knows no bounds. It was asked with a dismissive derisive tone.

Friends, we are here tonight, not merely to grieve and to embrace the death that comes. We are here tonight because, even in the face of suffering we have an answer to Pilate. We know truth. We are not arrogant enough to claim possession of absolute truth, but we do know this. We know that truth lives, breathes, and grows in the building of life-giving, authentic human community. We know, even in the darkness of the tomb, that there is truth found in the integrity of human relationships. We know, even in the terror and the torture, that in compassion there is truth. We know that all the yelling and spewing of hatred and bigotry cannot erase the power of self-giving love.

We are here tonight to feel the pain of loss, it's true. But in that pain we reach for one another and claim the truth that is love, the truth that is hope, the truth that is the new life we know will come among us. So let us on this night of darkness clasp one another's hands and dare to answer Pilate when asks us....What is truth?

Amen.

Resurrection of the Lord
John 20:1-18 or Luke 24:1-12

Resurrecticity

I want to tell you a story this morning about this woman who went out and bought herself a parrot. This woman's name was Erma, and Erma wanted in the worst way to have a bird that talked. She went to the pet store and selected what was a pretty costly bird. She took the bird home and waited for it to speak. Nothing happened. So she went to the pet shop and told the storekeeper that the bird didn't talk. "Well," said the man, "Why don't you take home this mirror and put it in the bird's cage? They like to look at themselves and sometimes that helps them talk. Home she went to give the mirror a try.

A few days later she was back at the store again. "The mirror didn't work," she announced with her jaw a little tense. "Okay," said the pet store owner, "Why don't you take this bell and hang it in the cage? Sometimes they like the sound of the bell and that helps them begin to talk." So Erma headed home with the bell only to return a few days later. This time her irritation was beginning to show. The edge could be heard in her voice as she said, "The bird still won't talk." "Okay, okay," said the store owner. "Try this little ladder for him. Maybe he just needs the exercise."

A few days later the woman was back in the shop again. This time she marched right up to the counter and loudly announced that her parrot had died. The clerk looked at her quizzically and said, "Died? Really? What happened? Did you ever get him to talk?" "Yes," said Erma with real sadness in her voice. "Well," said the clerk, "What did he say? What were his last words?"

Erma frowned and said, "Hey, don't they have any food at that pet shop?"

Yes, yes, yes! It's a terrible story, I know! I still like it, though. And the truth is that I like this story because it kind of mirrors our lives a bit. We spend so much time running around attending to things that we think are important as we often fail to go deeply into the things that really matter.

It's like having a whole bag of rubber bands and not knowing that their principle quality is that they stretch. Can you imagine holding a rubber band in your hand and being clueless about the fact the thing stretches out like this (*stretch rubber band in hand*). Yes indeed, rubber bands have what my dictionary refers to as "elasticity." It is, in other words, the character of a rubber band to be elastic. But if we don't take that rubber band and wrap it around a pile of envelopes or files, or shoot it mischievously at our little sister, it's not of much use, is it?

It has that quality of stretching. In our language that suffix or word ending is attached to an adjective, turning it into a noun focusing on the character, essence or substance of the noun.

It occurs to me that you may be thinking that you didn't come here on this Easter Sunday to get an English grammar lesson, but bear with me as we go back to Erma and her parrot.

Unfortunately, Erma did not have what? "Bird-ici-ty?" In other words, she did not understand the character or essence of having a bird in the house. Thus, she didn't realize that it wouldn't live, much less talk, without food.

Think about it. A rubber band, as we have made clear, has *elasticity*. We know and understand this. Then of course there is *electricity*, which in my feeble understanding is the movement of electrons in a particular sort of way. We understand the character of these electrons well enough to make use of them in a million different ways. Then we come to *simplicity*, which points us to the core or essence of being simple. If only we could focus on that in the midst of our over work and over busy lives, we would be healthier and less stressed. Another "icity" word that comes to mind is *authenticity*, which is the character of being authentic or real. If we could locate and live into authenticity in our lives, a lot of things would be different, don't you think?

There are a lot of words in the English language that have this "icity" suffix.

Here are just a few.

allergenicity
analyticity
anthropocentricity
apostolicity
aromaticity

Friends, I have been thinking a lot about this as we have walked together into the thicket of Easter celebration. My thinking and my praying have caused me to consider the concept of "resurrecticity." When it comes to the notion of the resurrection I think that we sometimes resemble Erma in her drive to get that parrot to talk. I don't need to tell you that the resurrection of Jesus Christ is at the core of our faith, and yet we so often dance together around the edges of resurrection reality. We don't, in other words, go deeply into the character and essence of the reality of resurrection. We don't get "resurrecticity."

A rubber band stretches.

Electrons flow.

Simplification reduces stress

And authenticity builds trust.

But what of the resurrection?

What is *resurrecticity*?

Many, of course, focus on the historical event. Thousands of people have tried to find the original shroud and the market in allegedly genuine artifacts is always good. Indeed, the Shroud of Turin to this day draws hordes of tourists to examine the alleged burial shroud of Jesus. Others prefer to think of as a myth, which tends to blunt the power of it all by dismissing it as a mere story. Still others move into the powerful realm of metaphor, living into the truth and poetic power of new life. And then there are some who just shrug it off and refused to deal with it.

No matter how we approach this it feels important to live together into what it would mean to have "resurrecticity" in our lives. I believe that there is a deep and wonderful reason for us to consider the character and substance of the resurrection as we claim this centerpiece of Christian faith.

This morning the cross is empty. We sing "Christ The Lord Is Risen Today." We fill our Easter baskets.

We live out a many layered tradition around this Easter business, going deeply together into the depth and meaning of it all.

Resurrecticity? What is it? What does it mean? I know. There are many people with more clarity and knowledge than me, but I'd like to suggest this much.

Resurrecticity is the act of living into the assumption that new life is not only possible but present at this very moment.

Reurrecticity is the willful and intentional living into a practiced naiveté that assumes the best about people and cuts their well-honed cynicism.

Resurrecticity doesn't check to see if someone follows the same party line or ideology as you, but instead celebrates differences and builds authentic community on the strength of those differences.

Resurrecticity practices compassion and forgiveness.

Resurrecticity seeks and develops joy. Resurrecticity envisions and risks a better tomorrow.

My hope, dear friends, is that we will walk from this place today invested in going deeper. My prayer, sisters and brothers, is that we will live together into "resurrecticity" and explore the substance, death and character of the resurrection of Jesus Christ and what it means in our lives and in our church.

Let us begin this deepening journey as we stand in awe before an empty cross. Let us be in joyful prayer as we engage together in "resurrecticity."

Amen.

Easter 2
John 20:19-31

Poor Old Thomas

Well, it's over. The eggs have been hidden and glee-
fully found. The leftovers are mostly eaten. Family vis-
its are complete and we're all looking forward to warm
weather — and to settling back into our routines. This
whole Easter celebration thing is a little bit tiring, don't
you think? I note that a few folks have chosen to stay
home this Sunday. Don't worry. I am not trying to mention names or point fingers! In fact, many pastors take
this Sunday off after this time of intensity and worship.
Who doesn't, after all, need a break, even from church?

It's true. Everyone gets to take a break now and
then, even your pastor! But I wonder if this lull following the celebration of the resurrection might be about
something more than just being a bit tired? Could it be
that there may be something subtle working in all of us
that makes it tough to face church on the Sunday after
Easter Sunday? Do you think we could we find and explore what might be described as a kind of post-Easter
timidity?

Think back to what is happening in this scripture
today. We have a whole crew of Jesus' followers gathered together in a place of relative safety. It's probably
not an exaggeration to suggest that they were not exactly running around shouting joy to the storm. Just
look at them! Behind locked doors and trembling in

fear, it's a bit of a stretch to believe that they were witnesses to the risen and living Lord. And in my own mind, this is where Thomas gets a raw deal.

Usually, we read this scripture while wagging a finger at poor old "Doubting Thomas." Most of us, I think unconsciously, picture ourselves as one of the good guys shaking our head at a Thomas who demands proof of Jesus' resurrection. We step away in vague embarrassment from a Thomas who is too weak to accept the reality of new life in Christ Jesus. Is that true for you? I know it is for me. I read this story and hear the words of Jesus, who says, "Blessed are those who have not seen and yet believe." And I think to myself, "Boy do I feel bad for the Thomases of the world." Though this is my inside voice, which no one actually hears, I must confess that in my thoughts the tone is one of judgment, and even superiority.

It's tough to step back and think about a bigger picture here. Could it be that there's more going on here than the machinations of a cynic who needs proof? Maybe, just maybe Thomas is the only brave one in the bunch. Maybe Thomas is voicing feelings that no one else has the nerve to articulate?

I once had a friend who had this quality. The truth of the matter is that he was a generally unpopular guy. He was one of those people who could come up with questions and comments that were, well, embarrassing. He would ask that question that somehow was on everyone's mind but no one had the courage to actually say the words. This did not faze John. One time we went together to a concert of *avante garde* music. This music was truly out there, and unlike anything most of us would identify as music. After the concert, we all attended the reception where the composer of this music was holding court. We stood, nodding politely while the musician discussed his music and explained what he was trying to express with it. Suddenly John piped up and said, "I don't know. It kind of sounded like someone was trying to strangle a chicken." Silence — no one said a word.

After a moment, everyone started to make fun of John, chiding him because he didn't appreciate this wonderful eclectic music. The real truth, though, was that John had voiced the feeling of just about everyone in that room. What if this was the case with Thomas? I mean, it's all well and good to point the finger at the one who brazenly demands proof. It's another thing, however, to step back and look at the room full of people hiding out from the police like common criminals. Who are these people and what is their real story? If Jesus was truly risen from the dead; if these people really believed that, then what were they doing cowering behind locked doors in some out of the way room?

What I'm trying to think about with you is this. Is it possible that the sheer magnitude of the resurrection makes us a little queasy? Could it be that on this Sunday after Easter Sunday we too are hiding out in our own upper room? After all, the implications of all this are staggering. If we embrace this it will have a profound impact on our lives. Because this is a pretty big deal, I wouldn't mind actually seeing that wound, would you? Yet Thomas spared the crowd by asking the question that rested uneasily in everyone's spirit. Thomas wanted to know. Thomas wasn't afraid to find the truth. He wasn't afraid to demand proof, to literally challenge God.

Wow.

This doesn't mean we throw out the blessings that Jesus has for those who can believe without seeing. For this kind of vulnerability is also a piece of our calling. Yet, let's not forget that doubt, and the daring spirit to ask the question, to risk the knowing, is also an important part of our faith.

The philosopher Renes Descarte coined the phrase, "*Cogito ergo sum,*" which means "I think, therefore I am." But for we who follow the path of faith, one could articulate these words along with Thomas. "*Dubito ergo sum,*" or "I doubt therefore I am." Doubting is an essential part of faith. If we simply accept things as they are without asking the questions, without probing our own minds and hearts, then we cannot be very seriously pursuing faith. Today, let us give thanks for the Thomases in our lives. Today, let us acknowledge that without Thomas, those followers of Jesus might have stayed hidden in that room for quite a while. Think with me for a moment, about those people in your own lives who dare to ask the uncomfortable questions, who push the envelope, and who all the time are the ones who have the courage to ask the questions we are unwilling to utter.

And as we lift up poor old Thomas, let us claim that dynamic conversation of faith that includes doubt and certainty, questions and answers, and the willingness to share and love deeply.

Amen.

Feed My Sheep

I used to have this great old guitar. It was a "Harmony F-Hole, which was a copy of a much more expensive model, and it was old. I liked it, a lot. It had accompanied me on my many excursions into cafés and coffeehouses. It thumped around in the back of my old Subaru to church outings and late night jam sessions. It was, well, familiar. The varnish was all worn off on the neck and it was scratched and well-used. Again, I liked it. I liked it a lot.

Then one day, against my better judgment, I lent it to a friend who had a gig at a neighboring college. As I handed him the guitar case that day, I remember having one of those uneasy feelings in the pit of my stomach. Perhaps you have had such a feeling yourself at one time or another? It's one of those feelings that I frequently ignore, which says, "Don't do this. You'll be sorry if you do." So I ignore my inner voice as I shrug and say, "What could happen?"

The next day Larry showed up at my apartment without the guitar. I was thinking to myself, "this is not a good sign." He poured himself a cup of coffee and sat down. The silence was awkward. I looked him in the eye and I said, "Hi Larry, where's my guitar?" Larry looked up and said, "Boy, your guitar sure sounded good last night." I swallowed hard, searching for some patience, and asked again. "Larry, where's my guitar?" He shot back, a little testy this time. "You know, you had a few serious cracks in that instrument."

Had? Had? Past tense? Had a few serious cracks? I was seriously worried now and I asked one more time, "Larry, where's my guitar?" It was then that the painful truth emerged. During intermission, my guitar had fallen under the heel of a drunken bar patron who had wandered on the stage. It was, Larry, stammered out, "gone." A sad story. Did I tell you really liked that guitar?

Perhaps you know this story? I don't quite mean that you know these details, but I am wondering if the same personalized version of this tale has ever happened to you? Someone you know has done something about which they feel guilty. Each question you ask is deflected, and each interrogative is met with dissimilation, deft dodges, and a wily dance around the room. Does this sound familiar? It's a situation where the person with whom you are dealing will do almost anything to keep from answering your questions. Finally, the questions are repeated often enough that the dancer must stop and truly respond.

It reminds me of certain government officials who pass budgets with billions of dollars in increases for weapons of death but turn around quickly to say with a righteous twang that there's not enough money to pay for schools or highways or health care. When you try to pin them down about the obvious lie they dance and dodge and, like my friend Larry, try to do anything but tell the truth. Instead, we are fed platitudes about getting the government's hand out of your pocket, which is untrue and meaningless. And after wading through lie after lie, you fall down faint from confusion and dismay and you keep asking, again, and again. Why do we have enough money for death, but not for the things that improve and give life? Why? Why? Why?

Ah. I am seeing a glimmer of recognition on faces around the room. You do know it, don't you? It's that cyclic sliding thing, where real issues are avoided, where talk is shifted and subjects changed. It's a hazy twilight of untruth designed to befuddle and disempower, and we are up to our hips in it, in our personal lives, in our social lives and in our church.

But wait, because there is a note of hope in all this. When I pick up my Bible and read the gospel of John and see that good old Peter could dissimilate with the best of them, I breathe a little easier. Good old Peter. Peter and the gang.

After receiving instructions to go to Jerusalem and wait, they were, of course, not doing that. They were, instead, hanging out by the Sea of Tiberius. Jesus then showed up in one of what scholars like to call a "post-resurrection appearance, " and stood there shaking his head. Don't you love that? A "post-resurrection experience." It sounds more like a medical condition than the appearance of the risen Christ. My mind goes to the triage room at the local urgent care center. Someone is talking to the triage nurse. "Oh no! I've got a bad case of a post-resurrection experience! Will I survive?"

But I digress. Jesus showed up, and the guys were thinking fast about how to react to this Jesus who was supposed to be dead, when he came to take them fishing and then invited them to breakfast. We cannot know this, of course, but I can imagine Peter's panicked thought process as his eyes darted back and forth between Jesus and the rest of the disciples. His interior monologue wouldn't quit. "So far so good. Maybe this won't be so bad after all. Maybe this will be okay?

Then, as Peter completed his thought, Jesus leaned into the group and dropped the big one. He put his hand on Peter's shoulder and he posed this question.

"Do you love me?"

Of course, we know from scripture that this went down three times with the same answer issuing forth. Thanks, though to our own inept and agenda laden biblical translators, we completely miss the power of what was going on in this exchange. You see, the questions and the answers are actually a bit different than what we read here. In fact, it was rather more like Larry and my guitar.

Jesus asked the question, "Do you love me?"

Our first assumption here is that this is an interpersonal exchange. Do they love Jesus?" But the Greek word translated here as "love" is "*agape*." This is not a term that refers to one person loving another. It refers instead to a love that is whole and total; a love that requires the well-being of neighbors and enemies; a love that can only exist in the context of authentic community. And Jesus wasn't concerned with how they felt about him particularly. He wanted to know if his followers were able to participate in agape love. So he posed the question: Do you love in this way? Do you love with agape love? Do you love with a love that reaches past self and into community?

Peter, to whom the question was not addressed, jumped in and said, "sure, I love you." But he didn't respond with the word "agape." He instead responded with the Greek, "*philio*," which means brotherly love. Or perhaps in a more contemporary rendering it could mean "buddies." "Sure, man, I love ya…." This is substantially different than "agape love." *Philio* is an individualistic affection. It is defined and categorized as a kind of caring with specific limits and mutually understood boundaries. It is manageable.

It's me, loving the guy down at the deli because he is a pretty good guy. It's you, nodding at the ticket taker at the train station. It could be anyone in your circle. *Philio* remains safe and controllable. As such, there's nothing wrong with this kind of affection. It's fine, as far as it goes. It's just not the focus or intent of Jesus' teaching and ministry.

As we peel away the linguistic problems of scripture, we find that Jesus was not simply trying to irritate the disciples by repeating a question they already answered. Instead, he was asking a penetrating, life altering question: "Will you participate in agape love? Will you wholly and totally love? Will you love your enemies and pray for those who persecute you? Will you love with a love which can transform and heal? Will you love each and every person, not as you wish they were, but as they really are? As God created them?

And like the disciples, we too try to avoid going deep. "Hey," we say, "Chill out, Jesus! We already said we are you're good buddies."

But Jesus didn't buy the dodge. He kept asking, now as then, "Do you love me? Will you commit yourself and give yourself fully in authentic Christian community? Will you stop dancing and dissimilating? Will you listen and love, not with some neat categorical affection that can be controlled and portioned out….

but with a love which is free and freeing?

Will you love with a love that is greater than the sum of all our parts?

A love that calls us together as a people?

A love that opens the doors of the church to all people, not matter who they are or where they've been in life?

Friends, the painful truth for us is that Jesus has had to go on asking through the centuries, "Do you love me? Today this question comes to us. Will we look down and mutter like my friend Larry and answer a question that has not been asked? Will we spin out elaborate untruths about some trifling and transitory affection? My own answer to this question is a resounding, "No!" No. I think that in this Easter season this church, this people will rise with Christ to give the answer he was seeking all the time.

Together, we will answer, "Yes Lord, we promise to build a community based on agape love. Yes Lord, we will love openly and widely as we create a loving community. Yes God, we are not playing around anymore. Today, with all the saints gathered here we commit anew to giving our time, our energy, our inner strength, our full selves to the work of the agape community. Yes God, we will feed your sheep,

Amen.

Everything You Do Bears Witness

I remember once a few weeks ago, I was having a bad day. Have you ever had a bad day? Bad days can cover a pretty wide arc of human reality, but my day began with not being able to find my bedroom slippers. Then, as soon as I got in the shower, someone downstairs ran the dishwasher and I was suddenly receiving cold water therapy at no extra charge! Then I tripped getting out of the shower and broke the table in the bathroom. Once I was out of the shower and shivering, I reached for clothing, only to discover that the shirt I pulled from the closet had a stain on it. I know. These are what my children would call "first world problems." Suffice it to say, I was pretty grumpy.

Downstairs the coffee was cold and I was sitting at the kitchen table muttering some string of unacceptable epithets. My wife came in from her walk and asked, "What's wrong?" I turn my head to meet her gaze. "What's wrong? Why nothing, nothing at all. I'm fine."

She continued to gaze at me, shaking her head and she said with a faint smile. "Right."

My eyes popped open and I said, "What do you mean? I said I'm fine so what's wrong?"

This person has been with me for many years and she just shook her head, kissed me on the forehead, and said, "Let me know when you want to talk." I didn't really have to say anything. My spouse of 25 years knew instantly that something was bothering me. My grumpy demeanor and my actions had given me away.

Actions, as we are told, speak louder than words. This is such a well-worn axiom that it could be relegated to the level of a cliché. It is, however, a true statement, and one that is brought up powerfully for us in the gospel of John today. Here we see the writer of John calling us to examine this cliché up close and personal. Today we are not asked to review a lengthy resume' outlining what is done by this Jesus fellow. In fact, the whole question really gets turned around a bit because the reality is that we have a guy here who is strangely reluctant to talk too much about himself or his ministry.

Yes. I know. Scriptures actually have Jesus saying quite a lot, don't they? I am not saying that he was particularly quiet in the sense of talking and sharing. In fact, in my mind's eye I see Jesus with his head reared back, caught in the midst of a powerful laugh. He was maybe sitting at the table with all the wrong kinds of people; the kind I wouldn't let my kids talk to, and he heard a joke or a comment, and he laughed. This laughter was pure, free, and open to the power of the fellowship. So, from my own perspective it's not that he was withdrawn or introverted. It was really that he didn't talk much about himself. When it came to his miracles and the things he was teaching his followers he would tend to get a little more circumspect. In fact, the gospel record shows a number of occasions when Jesus told his disciples and others not to tell anyone about what they had heard and seen. Biblical scholars even call it the "Messianic secret."

In this reading we find Jesus in Jerusalem cornered by the religious authorities. If he was a member of my United Methodist tribe, he would be in the room with Bishops and Superintendents and staff from the Annual Conference. And what was it these people wanted? They did not want him to offer proof of anything. At least they didn't ask for that. They didn't wish him to back up his stories, and they didn't really want him to repeat one of his miracles. Instead they asked him when he was going to make the announcement. When, they wanted to know, will you let *us* know that you are the Christ?

What a question to ask. It's like being a firefighter who is walking away from the scene of a big fire that has just been extinguished, and as you climb into your truck people gather around to ask when you will let them know you are a firefighter.

So what did Jesus say? The obvious thing, I guess. He said, "I told you. You just don't want to believe it. Everything I do bears witness to me. But you won't believe it." One has to wonder what it was about the announcement that these people felt they needed?

Imagine if someone approached you and said, "When are you going to let us know if you're a Christian or not?" How would this make you feel? Suspicious? Wary of a trap perhaps? Indeed, what they were looking for was Jesus to actually say the words. When he made the public announcement they would then have the goods on him. He could teach and do miracles all around the countryside but these people wanted the words out of his own mouth to convict him. It was similar as Jesus stood before Pilate while he asked him if he was king of the Jews. Jesus replied, "You say that I am" (John 18:37).

The thing we need to keep clear about is that now, as then, we live in a world littered with words. In the present circumstances in our nation these words contradict, conflict, and give false witness every day. Increasingly, in our contemporary morass, we can say pretty much whatever we want. Statements and observations no longer have to have any shred of connection to truth or reality. We can, simply, say whatever we wish and call anyone with a different view a liar. It's in moments like this that we need to remember that what we do bears witness to us and to our Lord. It reminds me of an old friend who would frequently wonder out loud as he glanced sideways at me, saying, "If you got arrested tomorrow for being a Christian, would there be enough evidence to convict you?" In the case of Jesus there was ample evidence to convict, but he refused to play their language games. Instead, he just insisted that the authorities simply look at his actions.

As I listen to the way in which the cultural wars have invaded the fabric of Christian community and we become chained to our ideological positions of being liberal or conservative or left or right, I hear the same questions boomerang back to us. While we are pretty certain that we are not the Messiah, the question of authenticity follows us in much the same way it did Jesus. They wanted to know. Was he the Messiah, yes or no? And today people ask us. Are we Christians or not? Are we? Do we follow Jesus? Or have we been reduced to knee-jerk reactionaries who issue forth from religiously tainted outlets for the shrill banter of the left and the right?

If we truly follow Jesus then let our lives be our witness. Let everything we do speak to the world around us and let us continually ask ourselves this significant question. If this is what we profess, would there indeed be enough evidence to convict us? Would our lives give testimony to what we profess? Or would we leave behind us a trail of secular, ideological bickering that hampers our ministry and our witness?

So it is that at the end of the day I am not overly concerned with what people say they believe. We know, don't we, that people say all kinds of things? For my money I don't need to hear a list of beliefs, doctrines, or rules. Show me your life and I will know very clearly what it is you believe.

Jesus said, "Everything I do bears witness to me." Yes, yes, yes. It's not just Jesus but we who claim to follow him. Everything we do bears witness to who we say we are as a people of faith. Let's think back 24 hours. Has everything you've done borne witness to the love of Jesus? Everything? Really? I know that I was driving home last night and this guy cut me off at a stop light. The hand gesture I offered him definitely did not give witness to the love of Jesus.

One of the profound things that happens in owning this is that we have, in effect, taken down the walls of our local church. *Everything* we do bears witness. Everything we do at the supermarket, at work, or on the road — everything. We can no longer come to our sanctuaries and act religiously for an hour or so before going back to business as usual. In this moment we are called to a new level of committed, intentional living. Everything we do bears witness to Jesus, and that, friends, calls us out of this building so that we can be the church together.

My hope and my prayer is that we will open our arms wide and sing praises to a wonderful God as we live out our faith today, tomorrow, and the day after that in the name of Jesus Christ.

Amen.

Death Shall Be No More

Every once in a while something happens that totally shifts the landscape of our perceptions. Every once
in a while something profound takes place that makes
all our old discussions and ways of understanding
move to a new location. Examples abound in history.

Life after Mr. Watt's steam engine was different forever. The invention of the assembly line catapulted us
into an economic world that, for good and ill, shapes
our lives even in this moment. Even in the polarized
climate in our nation today, we can look with pride at
the two-term presidency of the first African-American
to hold that office! This doesn't mean that we are done
dealing with the horrors of racism and bigotry — far
from it. But the election of Barack Obama is one of
those moments. Things have changed.

Each one of us can likely point to other historic
shifts. The arrival of the automobile, the computer, fast
food, driverless cars; the list is long. In my own faith
community it can be said without fear of contradiction
that the arrival of Mr. Wesley and his Methodists was a
moment like that. John Wesley and his potent blend of
deep piety and an unwavering commitment to social
justice left an indelible mark on the world stage, from
scores of schools, universities, and hospitals to literally millions of people whose hearts were "strangely

warmed" by a gospel that was freed from the straight jacket of rigid doctrine and made accessible by this laity led movement and their saddleback preachers.

Today, because of these Methodists and their restless activism, child labor laws are on the books in this country. It was because of the bold leadership of bishops like Francis J. McConnell that the tyranny of the McCarthy era in this nation came to a close. For Methodists of that day and this, the call is to stand on new ground, preaching and living the gospel. Indeed, this call comes to all Christians.

"See," wrote John of Patmos, "I am making all things new."

In Revelation, the writer is speaking on a grand and universal scale. This apocalyptic writing isn't about one invention or one people changing things. He was writing of a time of cataclysmic change. He was writing in the context of Roman occupation and rebellion; a time of epic and catastrophic change; a time when he envisioned all things being made new. A new Jerusalem would emerge in the midst of joy and wonder. It would be a time when every tear shall be wiped from our eyes and death will be no more....for the former things will have passed away.

The book of Revelation and its apocalyptic warnings and visions can be scary things to ponder. It's no wonder that people of questionable ethics and mental balance have turned to this book to spout manic pictures of fire and brimstone. We have heard it before, and having heard it, we react by dismissing the text. Preachers, theologians, and pew sitters try to ease the pinch of Revelation by saying that "we all have apocalypses in our lives." The well-intended intent is to scale down the towering implications of these writings by confining them to personal pietistic ramblings while we comfortably ignore the words and the context of Revelation.

So, let us make all things new and forget the televangelists. Let us imagine anew the scripture unfettered by those who would manipulate, not only the text, but faith itself for their own ends. Let us begin anew and let go of former impressions as we prayerfully consider a world where all things are indeed made new! Let us envision a world where death is no more; a reality where God's home is not in the clouds but here among us!

For me, this scripture gains clarity when viewed through the lens of this passage from the gospel of John.

"I give you a new commandment, that you love one another. Just as I have loved you, you should also love another. By this everyone will know that you are disciples, if you have love for one another."

I know that this doesn't sound particularly apocalyptic does it? In fact, we know this routine. We know the drill. Sure, Jesus said we are to love one another. He wants us, in other words, to play nice. But down deep we know it's more than good manners on the playground. It's more than a formula for getting through this life in relative comfort. Jesus wants love to be the core of our identity. This is how people will know we are disciples; by the way we love. Not by our jobs or status or economic location; not our accomplishments or even by our carefully rehearsed piety, but by our love.

Here in the Gospel of John and throughout our Christian scriptures I believe we are being called to a kind of love that places us on new ground. This is a love that is bigger than a steam engine, bigger than the assembly line or any human invention. It's larger than computers and fast food, even larger than our denominational identity! I want to say today that these icons and accomplishments are the former things that will pass away in the tidal wave of love that we are called to in Christ Jesus.

This is a world-changing love. It is a love that seizes us and jolts us out of our comfort zones, placing us on the street with a God who wants us to love so powerfully and fully that this love will become our identity. It will be the way in which we are known.

Sisters and brothers, right now we are not known by our love.

If you ask people about Christians, if you ask the world out there how we are known, some not very flattering answers will come our way. Christians in the so-called "popular" culture are known, not for love but for rigidity. Christians are known, not for love, but for judgment and exclusivity. In my own United Methodist community we are known for our intra-Nicene bickering about whom we will consider to fully welcome in the church. We are known less by our love and more by the ways in which we have taken on the values of this world as we face off between liberal and conservative, left and right.

But friends, in Christ Jesus we are called to put on a new ID Badge. In God's love we are called to move out from the haze of the "former things," and to make all things new with the lived love of God in our lives, our church, our community and our world.

You see, this love, if we will fully give ourselves to it, will indeed end the world as we know it. This love, if we live it fully and uncompromisingly, will indeed wipe away ever tear. This love, if we embrace it and move in its power, will not end death itself for that is the marvelous way of creation. All living things die. Let us meet our passing, when it comes, with grace and thanksgiving. But when the scriptures speak about the vanquishing of death, let us hear this spoken of in terms of the ways of death, the culture of death. Let us rise up in love to do away with the way of violence, oppression, and coercion, the ways of hurt and wounding, the ways of manipulation and greed.

Love, you see, is the apocalyptic button we need to push.

"Then I saw a new heaven and a new earth..."

This is a heaven and earth where people meet one another without suspicion or anger. A place where competition and hard-hearted individualism gives way to a community of compassion and justice. Let us live into a new Jerusalem. Let us live together into a kind of love that will become our identity. Let us step into the world changing role of a people who love radically, a people who give, not just generously, but fully and completely of ourselves.

Let us stand above the ashes of the way things used to be and build a new world where we are defined, not by conflict or possessions, not by ideology or political leanings but by the full and courageous living out of the love we have received from God in Jesus Christ.

Amen.

Easter 6
John 14:23-29 or John 5:1-9

Not As The World Gives

I remember when our twins were infants we lived in a third floor walkup in Greenwich Village in New York City. One day I decided to give my wife a break and take the kids out for a stroll in our neighborhood. With twins there is a certain amount of baggage required when you head out the door. Stroller built for two? Check. Diaper bag with snacks and so on? Check. Bottles of formula and other necessities? Check.

Carrying two, active ten-month-old babies and navigating down the stairs with all that stuff was, well, it wasn't actually possible. I was beginning to grasp this as I stood on the stoop looking helpless and trying to figure out what to do. Should I put the kids down and unfold the stroller? That didn't seem like a great idea. Should I go back upstairs and leave things on the landing and then take the kids down one at a time? No, leaving one child alone on the sidewalk struck me as a bad idea. Just as I was beginning to see the utter futility in all this, something amazing happened.

This woman, who I knew from our local neighborhood, and with whom I frequently chatted, came strolling down the street. She took one look at me in my quandary and came bounding up the steps. "How are you pastor?" She quipped as she took diaper bag and stroller from me. "It looks like you could use a hand.

I raised four kids in a walkup like this." She promptly unfolded the stroller and waited for me to bring the kids down to buckle them in for the ride ahead. As soon as that was done she waved and went on her way. It happened so fast I hadn't absorbed it all. Who was that masked woman?

As I headed down our street I couldn't help marveling. Here, seemingly out of nowhere, was a person who saw me struggling and was able to identify with me. Here was someone with the presence of mind to simply stop and be of some assistance. A sense of gratefulness flooded my spirit.

Has anything like that ever happened to you? You're all bound up, caught in the web of too many things and too much to do; you're filled up with the rush and crush of all that the world demands; or maybe this is just a tough moment; a window of painful aloneness, and suddenly someone is there. Suddenly someone appears who understands, who has somehow shared your experience and is able to touch your feelings and your anxiety, your frustration and your hurt. And just as suddenly that someone steps up and offers him or herself. It may be as simple as helping a befuddled dad down the stairs — or it could be much deeper.

It is called empathy.

Jesus said, "Peace I give to you, my peace I leave with you. Not as the world gives do I give to you."

What I hope to reach for today is some understanding that we might share about this peace, this peace of Christ. This is the peace that passes all understanding. This peace, which heals all wounds and binds every heart, this peace that Jesus leaves, is left with the hope of uncovering our innate capacity to feel and understand what others are experiencing.

This is not the quick and thoughtless assumption that your experience must be what is happening to everyone else. This doesn't involve our arrogant projection of our own vision and desires onto the rest of the world. And this definitely does not tie into the prevailing narcissism of our culture which drones on and on about how the world should meet our own personal needs.

No.

The peace of Christ, the peace which Jesus leaves us is rooted in a selflessness which opens the heart to the experience of the other. This empathy, this engagement has to do with the ability to literally feel what people around you are feeling, to stand in someone else's shoes and become part of their experience. This is our ideal. This is our clear and stated vision. This is the place where hope takes shape.

However, the voice of the cynic is loud in the land and it gets expressed in seemingly endless lines of queries that go something like this:

"How am I supposed to know what someone else is feeling?" "I've never done this or been there." "I've never been a parent." "I don't know about that." "I've never been a student. I've never stayed up all night studying or worrying about loans or about a crazy professor who decided for some reason that he doesn't like me."

The questions keep coming, don't they?

"What do you want from me?" "I have never been in a relationship before." "How can you ask, how can you assume that I feel this or understand that?" "You ask too much — too much." And with apparent good intentions these same people will turn and say that it's not possible for one person to know how another feels. They can't possibly identify with them because their feelings are property upon which we do not trespass.

Friends, to all of you touched by this smog of cynicism I insist today that this is not merely possible, it is our calling. It is indeed possible to let go of preciously held selves and imagine what it must be like to be someone else. It is possible to move beyond the narrow limits of our own desires and become open to the power of the Spirit as it gives the gift of empathy and compassion. It is possible, and again, it is our call to open our hearts and our minds to include the experience of others into our consciousness.

The peace of God in Christ Jesus is this peace. It is quietude, a humility, an openness, a sensitivity which lets the old self die and raises up a new self, rooted and nourished in God's love. This peace removes our cultural obsession with me - me - me - me and faces it outward in active, self-giving love.

"My peace I leave with you, not as the world gives do I give..."

The peace of the world is the peace of selfishness, of insisting on one's own way, and upon one's own perspective as normative. The peace of the world is a peace built upon the assumption that my hurt and pain is all that matters and whatever I do to take care of myself is justified. This is a peace that is enforced; a peace that builds weapons and prepares for wars. It is the peace of presidents and kings and dictators. It is the peace of brittle alliances and clown-like juggling of power. This is the peace of an idolatrous culture which says that you can't love someone else until you love yourself.

Friends, today we come to abandon the peace of this world and to receive the peace that Christ brings. This peace of Christ surrenders the self and opens the cosmic heart to the reality of the other. It opens us to the pain of strained and broken relationships. It opens us to the struggles of someone who is out of work; it opens us to the heartache of loss and grief; to the passions through which each life journeys. It even opens us to the confused and frustrated look of a father standing on a Greenwich Village stoop.

My peace I leave with you; My peace I give to you. Not as the world gives do I give to you.

Amen.

The Difference Between
Happiness And Joy

I wonder if any of you have ever experienced joy. When I wonder this I do so with the clear intention of separating joy from happiness. The Constitution of our nation, while not guaranteeing us happiness, does guarantee us the right to chase after it. As a people, we are allegedly free to do whatever we wish to get that which makes us happy. And in the mind of this preacher, this promise of happiness has shaped us, and not in some good ways. So I ask, what is happiness? And how is it different from joy?

Happiness touches us at certain transitory levels. Chocolate ice cream makes me very happy. My morning walk with my dog makes me happy. A really great hot shower after a workout makes me happy. Watching movies makes me happy. What would be on your list of things that make you happy? Listening to Garrison Keillor on reruns of "A Prairie Home Companion" makes me happy. I could go on, because in truth, I find delight or happiness in many places.

But what about joy? Joy, it seems to me is quite different than happiness. Joy has a quality of being more consuming. That chocolate ice cream that makes me happy does not deter from the work at hand. Ice cream makes me happy and not much changes. However, a visit from one of my children brings deep joy and the capacity to drop whatever I'm doing to receive the blessing of being with them if only for a short while. You see, my family brings me true joy. Chocolate ice cream makes me happy. Joy has to do with the abandonment of the moment for a transcendent exultation about something which is deep or life transforming.

Music, for example, brings me joy. Music can transport me to a completely different, transformative place. It can even bring me closer to some piece of the holy. Music brings me joy. Having four guitars makes me happy. I wonder if you can summon up things from your own journey that fall into these two places. What are the things that make you happy? Binge-watching your favorite television show on a day off? Working in the yard? Riding your bicycle? Cooking your favorite dish for dinner? Sitting on the beach? You get to name the things that bring you happiness, and in our present reality you have the opportunity to pursue those things.

But joy? Joy is not something for which one prepares or works to attain. "Joy," as the psalmist said, "comes in the morning (Psalm 30:5)." It comes unbidden and often unexpected. The disciples were hardly expecting to witness the ascension of Jesus as we experience it in the gospel passage. Yet after witnessing this incredible thing they "returned to Jerusalem with great joy."

What, one wonders, were they joyful about, anyway? Perhaps they felt joy at the surprise of seeing their risen Lord? Maybe in the ascension there is an irrefutable witness to the reality of the Messianic claim. Or maybe the joy erupted out of the reality of the resurrection and the incredible implications that that has for all of creation.

Happiness can be attained while everything around you remains in relatively good order. But joy disrupts. Happiness is wonderful but being happy won't change much, except add pounds in the case of chocolate ice cream. Joy is not controllable. It slops over the sacred bowl in abandon, spilling the soup everywhere. Happiness is controllable. Indeed, if we do not keep our happiness and pursuit of it under control we are judged to be unwell, or even worse.

Joy has the power to change things. It is a joyful people who envision new possibilities. It is a joyful community that can see a future not yet built and move together in its construction. It is a joyful, worshiping people who receive God's transformational spirit into their lives, inviting God to change them as God sees fit.

After church today we will be having a wonderful potluck luncheon, which will make your pastor very happy! I treasure the family recipes and cultural richness that is revealed when we are at table together. I love the way we celebrate and the times we hold each other close when hard times or tragedies strike. One has to wonder if all these things I like about our community add up to joy in the long haul? Maybe — maybe that's so.

I would still suggest to us, though, that joy is deeper and more profound than happiness. Joy permeates our being and changes us. Joy calls us into a visionary future. Joy invites us to change the world and to be changed in the process. Joy comes when, at the end of a horrific struggle like seeing your Master murdered, you discover that he did not die after all, but has risen from the dead! Joy pushes and pulls us to imagine a world ruled, not by death, but by the joyful transformative power of new life in Jesus Christ.

As we join the disciples this day in witnessing the ascension of our Lord, may we reach to claim the joy that they claim as they head to Jerusalem. Together, may we breathe in the joy of new life as we build community and serve others in Jesus' name. And as the joyful followers of Jesus may we follow the disciples into the city with joy and healing for the whole world. Amen.

Partners With The Divine

Today I am thinking about what it means to be partners. For me, the first person that comes to mind when I think about this is my spouse. I am beyond blessed to have someone who is, in every way, a partner in life. We share the joys and the sorrows, the struggles and the laughter, and we take responsibility for our own behavior while making sure we "have each other's back." This is a partnership where it's possible to sit for hours in a room together, each with a book to read. No words are shared. No preferences uttered or requested. We are, simply, together. A partnership like that is a beautiful thing indeed. And while you remain distinct individuals there is a powerful way in which you connect because you are bound in trust and common purpose.

Maybe you know a partnership like this in your life? I once knew two guys who owned a hardware business in upstate New York. They worked together for years in this small town, dispensing hammers, nails and whatever the community needed. Sure, they were friends, but it was more than that. On slow mornings at the store you would see them in their chairs on the front porch of the building sharing coffee and watching the town go by. These guys didn't actually talk much, but they communicated a lot. These guys didn't have lengthy discussions about business philosophy or other things. They just came together as partners to run a business and serve their community. And after long years of doing this they sold the business and both retired. They continued their porch sitting, though, until they both passed away just days apart.

What does it mean to be a partner?

We could easily go the legal, business route and get that pretty quickly defined. However, the kind of partnership we are talking about here is not a limited liability company or a corporation. No, we are talking about something rooted here in relationship. We are looking at something that is rooted in trust and faith. In many ways trust and faith come very close to meaning the same thing, but without either, partnerships are hard to build.

Human partnerships, in and of themselves, require both work and intentionality. It's hard to maintain a full partnership if you're not focused and sharing the same purpose.

Whether it's my spouse and me or my old friends who ran the hardware business, common purpose is important. This is not only true of human interaction, it's also true of our partnership with God. I know. Some of you are saying, "What? Partnership? With God? How does that work?" Well, it works in much the same way that a human partnership does.

God yearns for a partnership with us and invites us to be so close that, as this passage from John indicates, we are in and of one another. Wow. I hear the cynic in me saying, "I'm not sure I want to be that close to anyone, even if it is God." But that's the cynic's voice. The other voice that emanates from the heart is the one that seeks relationship and that searches for connection and finds fulfillment in mutuality. This voice comes from a seeker of the holy and welcomes God's grace as it invites us into full relationship or partnership with God.

If we are doing this partnership with God in a good way it is a relationship where we participate in one another's being. As Jesus prays in the garden he prays not only for unity for his followers but also for unity (or partnership) with God.

"As you, Father are in me, and I am in you, may they also be in us..."(John 17:21). Here is the outline for a partnership with the divine. It is not about one party or the other, so much as it is about the building of the kingdom. I know, for example, that my spouse and I are together, not only to fulfill one another, but to be a blessing to the world around us. I know that we are deeply linked in this common purpose, so much so that John's language makes sense.

Partnership with the divine goes beyond our religiosity. It is deeper than our play-acting at church and it is more powerful than our own private agendas. Like all good partnerships, this one comes to fruition in common purpose. When we partner with God to care for creation by working against pollution and environmental degradation, we are in common purpose with God. When we work together to feed the hungry and heal the sick we are in common purpose with God. When we give ourselves fully to the work of building open and inclusive community we are in common purpose with God.

What do you think? Is partnership with the divine something we could pursue together? As a Christian community in this time and place, what are some of the ways that we might find common purpose with God to such an extent that we can feel ourselves connected — a part of each other? Might we think together about our neighbors around our church? Who are these people? What do they need? How might we step forward with God to build relationships and to be a healing presence? And how might we shape our spiritual journey so that this partnership is strengthened? How is it that we come together in prayer and discipline? How do we shape our lives so that we are in God and God is in us and we come together in witness and service for the whole world?

I believe that in this moment we are called to a deeper relationship with God. Maybe we are even called into a partnership with trust, love and common purpose. Maybe, just maybe, at the end of the day our partnership with the divine will bear the fruit of healing, hope, and salvation.

Amen.

www.ingramcontent.com/pod-product-compliance
Lightning Source LLC
Chambersburg PA
CBHW070017110426
42741CB00034B/2079